BERNAL DÍAZ

Historian of the Conquest

BERNAL DÍAZ

Historian of the Conquest

BY HERBERT CERWIN

UNIVERSITY OF OKLAHOMA PRESS
NORMAN

By Herbert Cerwin

These Are the Mexicans (New York, 1947)
Bernal Díaz: Historian of the Conquest (Norman, 1963)

Copyright 1963 by the University of Oklahoma Press, Publishing Division
of the University. Composed and printed at Norman, Oklahoma, U.S.A.,
by the University of Oklahoma Press. First edition.

56967

CONTENTS

ILLUSTRATIONS

Map

PREFACE

WHEN as a youth I lived in Guatemala, Don Antonio Batres Jáuregui occasionally came to call at our home. My father said Jáuregui was a descendant of Bernal Díaz del Castillo, one of the great conquerors of Mexico and Guatemala. I remember that I looked upon Don Antonio with awe and fear.

Many years later when Nelson Rockefeller, then Co-ordinator of Inter-American Affairs, sent me to Mexico, I began to study the history of the country. Among the books I read was Genaro García's edition of Bernal Díaz' *True History of the Conquest of Mexico*. It was an exciting, dramatic book and Bernal Díaz fascinated me. I wanted to know more about him. He was a soldier in Cortés' army, but how did he happen to write a book which was still read four hundred years after his death? What was his background and what kind of a man was he? What happened to him after the Conquest?

I read everything available on Bernal Díaz, but found that the material in print was limited and often contradictory. Some authors reported that he began writing his *True History* at the age of eighty. One writer even questioned that Bernal Díaz participated in the Conquest. There was very little known about his married life and his children or why he left Mexico to reside in Guatemala.

Bernal Díaz was barely twenty-three years of age when in 1519 he came with Cortés from Cuba. His *True History* is not an autobiography, but an eyewitness account of the conquest of Mexico written long after he had taken part in it. It is gossipy, full of human interest, and it has by now become a classic. In writing it, Bernal Díaz revealed a great deal about himself, but he was quite evasive in describing many other important events in his life. He tells nothing of his early years and he hardly touches on the many years that were to follow, when, as a member of the *cabildo,* he took an active interest in the affairs of Guatemala.

He returned to Spain twice, but in his *True History* he is vague about these trips and the purpose behind them. He does not mention the letters of protest he wrote to the king or his fights with the clergy or the lawsuits in which he was involved. He virtually ignores the most fruitful years of his life.

Clearly there was a need for a biography that would comprehensively describe the story of his life and provide historians and the general reader with a better understanding of Bernal Díaz as well as the period in which he lived.

An opportunity to examine his life further came when I went to reside in Guatemala. Guatemala was where Bernal Díaz lived the major portion of his life and where he wrote his *True History*. In my search for information about him, the national archives in Guatemala proved to be a gold mine.

Carefully preserved documents dating back over four hundred years told in detail what transpired in the early days of the colony. In the dark and crowded rooms of the archives, Bernal

Díaz was no longer a vague figure of the past. As I read the *cabildo* records, he became alive and I could visualize him and almost hear him voicing his opinions about events taking place.

Slowly I began to piece together material about him. From one document the year of his birth was established; from another I learned whom he married, in what year, and how much he received in dowry; still another revealed that in addition to his large family, he also had three illegitimate children: two daughters and a son.

I learned that Bernal Díaz went to Spain as a lobbyist and that at one time he had to have the services of a bodyguard. I discovered how much income he received from his land. Yet he was constantly in debt, borrowing 350 *tostónes* on one occasion, and on another, as Christmas approached, the stout old warrior, now eighty-four, was in a holiday mood and wanted wine and suitable clothing material, so once more he borrowed money.

The records of the *cabildo* of which he was a member show his flourishing signature, vigorous and bold. But as death approached, he was able only to scrawl his initials. It was all there— as if he had signed the records yesterday.

Also in the Guatemala archives is what has always been considered the original manuscript of the *True History*. I was granted permission to photograph sections of it, and studies of the handwriting proved that the manuscript was not, as the Guatemalan government maintained, in Bernal Díaz' handwriting. Even his signature had been copied. This developed into something of a mystery that had to be clarified, which I have done in one of the chapters of this work. In all of this, my boyhood upbringing in the bilingual household of my parents in Guatemala has proved of inestimable value. The Spanish language is my language.

It was important to obtain some knowledge of the country

and terrain through which Bernal Díaz passed with Cortés. So, with friends, I traversed it, sometimes by jeep, other times on horseback and on foot. We went to the Río Dulce and then on to Honduras, in the heat and through the jungle. This trip turned into an experience we shall never forget—and proved to us what a remarkable group of men accompanied Cortés.

The research for and the preparation of this biography were carried out to gain a better insight into Bernal Díaz' life, his character, and the period in which he lived. To me, at least, Bernal Díaz is not dead, but very much alive. I trust that in reading this biography the reader will share this feeling with me.

Many persons made this book possible and among them I want to thank Professor Robert C. Padden of the University of California at Berkeley, who went over the manuscript and assisted in the preparation of the notes; Professor Lesley Byrd Simpson, also of the University of California, for providing material on Bernal Díaz; Frans Blom, archaeologist and Mayan trail blazer, now of San Cristóbal de las Casas; Padre Carmelo Santa Maria, S.J., of Madrid; Joaquín Pardo, director of the Guatemala archives; the late Sylvanus G. Morley; Edwin M. Shook, director of the University of Pennsylvania's Tikal Project; Darwin Teilhet of Los Altos, California; and my brother, Alfredo Cerwin of Guatemala. My deepest appreciation goes to my wife, Ruth Dagmar, who encouraged me in the writing of this book and accompanied me on horseback, by jeep, on foot, and by boat over the routes Bernal Díaz once traveled.

Herbert Cerwin

SAN FRANCISCO, CALIFORNIA
JANUARY, 1963

xii

BERNAL DÍAZ

Historian of the Conquest

1 ❧ "I WAS THERE . . .
   I SAW IT ALL . . ."

Lᴇss than an hour's drive from present-day Guatemala City, close to Volcanoes Fuego and Agua, lies the town of Antigua. The volcanoes and earthquakes, not time, have ravaged Antigua and left many of its once imposing buildings in ruins. But the lava which crumbled into soil centuries ago and the mild climate of a five-thousand-foot plateau make Antigua's *café en oro* one of the finest coffees in the world.

Antigua, the Old One, was given this name after it had been destroyed and abandoned. Although some of its inhabitants returned and buildings were rebuilt, it never regained its importance or former glory. Today it is a community with little activity and social life. Tourists go there primarily to visit the ruins and a few of the colonial buildings still standing. On market day, Indians descend from near-by villages to shop and to sell pottery and textiles. Every morning the church bells ring, calling the faithful to Mass, as they have done for over four hundred years.

In the sixteenth century, however, Santiago de los Caballeros de Guatemala, as the city was then called, was one of the leading Spanish settlements of the New World. It had a royal *audiencia,* directly responsible to the king, a bishop who spoke for the Church, and a *cabildo,* or city council, representing the people.

While the Spanish crown kept a tight control on its colonies, it made an earnest effort to permit the settlers to influence local affairs. The *cabildo* passed laws, saw to their enforcement, and openly protested when it felt that rulings from Spain were unfair and not in the best interests of the colonists.

The Guatemala *cabildo* held regular meetings, and detailed records reporting these council sessions are still in existence.[1] By going through these records, we find that the Spanish colonists in Guatemala at various periods of that century were having a difficult time. Even as today, they were confronted with the problems of high taxes, rising costs, and the threatening spiral of inflation.[2]

Members of the *cabildo* were called *regidores* and one of them, elected for life to the Guatemala *cabildo,* was Bernal Díaz del Castillo. By 1551, when this honor was bestowed upon him, he was fifty-four years of age and among the last of the surviving group of soldiers who had accompanied Cortés in that remarkable expedition which had brought about the conquest of Mexico.[3]

---

[1] *Actas del Cabildo,* Archivo del Gobierno de Guatemala (cited hereafter as AGG). The *Actas* are complete for two periods in the sixteenth century: from 1524 to 1530 and from 1555 to 1584.

[2] For a brilliant analysis of the economy, see Woodrow Wilson Borah, *New Spain's Century of Depression.*

[3] Although *cabildo* records are missing for this period, there is little reason to doubt this date, since Bernal Díaz himself gives it in a letter to the king in 1552. See Joaquín Ramírez Cabañas (ed.), *Historia verdadera*

The townspeople of the Guatemala colony looked upon Bernal Díaz as a prominent man who wrote letters to the king, occasionally acted as adviser to the governor, and over a bottle of Malaga liked to reminisce about the Conquest and the part he had taken in it. That he boasted and at times took more credit than was necessary was considered the prerogative of an old soldier.

For, while the conquest of Mexico had occurred some thirty-one years before, there were only a scattered few who remembered much about it. By 1550, the newer generation of settlers were more concerned with the present and the future than with the events of 1519. The daring strategy of Cortés and the valor of some four hundred Spanish soldiers who subdued the powerful armies of Montezuma were as vague to the townspeople as World War I is now to many citizens of the world.

Nevertheless, Bernal Díaz was a good storyteller and he had an unusual memory for detail and gossip. Many of his friends and some of the younger people enjoyed listening to him. They liked to hear him tell about Montezuma, how he bathed every day and never wore the same clothes a second time. He described the banquets Cortés gave and how on one occasion the guests stole the silver from the table. He related his suspicion that Cortés poisoned those who were sent to replace him and he even hinted that Cortés strangled his wife.[4]

But Bernal Díaz, despite his prominence in the affairs of the colony, was never looked upon as a scholar or a man of letters.

de la conquista de la Nueva España, por Bernal Díaz del Castillo (cited hereafter as Cabañas), III, 345. See also Antonio Fuentes y Guzmán, *Recordación florida del reyno de Guatemala,* I, 498.

[4] Bernal Díaz del Castillo, *Historia verdadera de la conquista de la Nueva España* (cited hereafter as BDC), *cap.* cxciv. This is Bernal Díaz' own manuscript and is kept in the AGG under the personal care of the director.

He had had a meager education and he knew only enough Latin to say his prayers; his knowledge of books and of the world was limited. He made no pretenses in this respect, in fact was the first to admit it.

On those occasions when he wrote to the king, or to members of the Council of the Indies, words and phrases came to him with difficulty. He considered himself principally a soldier, and while he was now a man of property and the head of a family with growing sons and daughters, he never thought of himself as anything else. Yet Bernal Díaz was to become famous and leave his mark on posterity as the author of the best eyewitness account we have of the Conquest.

Bernal Díaz was an excellent soldier. Without men such as he, Cortés might never have succeeded. Bernal Díaz took hardships, suffering, and defeat without protest, and with his tremendous energy he welcomed any challenge. But for years he was irked by the lack of recognition for himself and his fellow soldiers.

He felt that they had been ignored by the official reports, by the king, and by the Council of the Indies. Neither had he gained any of the riches he had been promised, and his letters and trips to Spain were prompted to obtain land grants. He and those who had fought in the conquest of Mexico had risked their lives and had not shared materially in any of the rewards or even in the glory. He was infuriated that only Cortés received the credit for defeating Montezuma's armies.

Bernal Díaz was convinced that unless the achievement of the soldiers was given full credit, the Spanish court and history itself would continue to ignore and dismiss the role they had played in the Conquest. People were quickly forgetting who had been responsible for making the colonization of the New World possible. Each ship brought more Spanish politicians with power to exploit land grants, though Bernal Díaz felt they had not earned the right to gain such royal favors.

Like many of the early Spanish settlers in the Guatemalan colony, Bernal Díaz was usually hard up financially. He enjoyed living well, and the land he owned and the produce which came from it were not always enough for his needs.

The letters of appeal Bernal Díaz wrote to Spain rarely brought action and generally went unanswered. For a long time he had mulled over the possibility of writing an eyewitness account of the Conquest. He put aside such a plan because he thought he did not have the ability and the scholarly talent necessary. He was reluctant to begin, despite the encouragement of his friends.

He maintained he could not express himself adequately nor did he have at his command the flowery prose of that era. He could not foresee that he would be included two hundred years after his death in the dictionary of the Royal Academy of Spain as one of the authorities of the Castilian language. Neither could he have guessed that, next to Cervantes, he would someday be the only other Spanish author so widely read abroad.

Between 1552 and 1557—the exact date is not known—Bernal, by then in his middle fifties, sat at a desk in his home and there reread and carefully studied Cortés' letters. They perhaps refreshed his memory, but these letters were not the only things which helped to recall experiences that had occurred more than a quarter of a century before.

In the room where he worked, there were souvenirs of campaigns of the type usually collected by soldiers. He had his swords, pieces of jade from Montezuma's treasury, and perhaps one or two mantles Montezuma had given him. We know he had a painting of an Aztec temple on the wall, for he describes it: "There are many paintings of temples in the possession of the conquerors, of which I have one, and those who have seen them will easily form an idea of the outside of this [Huitzilopochtli's] temple."

The house where Bernal Díaz lived and worked was a modest one. Part of it is still standing, though this is not the house so designated and generally shown to tourists. Bernal's home was located a short distance from the town square and was later rented to the Jesuits and became a part of their university.[5] Its style of architecture, like that of all the other homes, was a combination of Italian, Moorish, and Spanish. The windows were large, with turned-wood grilles and carved cedar shutters, and by one of these Bernal's wife must have sat in the late afternoon, according to custom, and watched the activities and sometimes processions which went on in the streets. Inside was the usual Spanish patio, and long halls with entrances to the various rooms. Somewhere in the house there was a shrine with a religious image and a wooden prayer pew for early-morning devotions.

The room where Bernal worked had a window to the street and from it he could see clearly the volcanoes in the distance. If by any chance his ghost had returned to haunt the place, it would have found Jesuit priests inhabiting the house and turning his former quarters into classrooms; today it is an abandoned building, with the courtyard used as a market place.

Bernal was to write three different prefaces for his work, but there is every reason to believe that the first words he wrote were

[5] Local records state that the Jesuits rented a house from the family of Bernal Díaz, and this house, likely as not, was the one originally belonging to Bernal Díaz and would have been located approximately where the market place of Antigua is today. Jesuit records exist in the Archivo General de las Indias, Seville, Spain (cited hereafter as AGI), Audiencia de Guatemala, 135.

"Bernal Díaz del Castillo, resident and *regidor* of this most loyal city of Santiago de Guatemala," and from there he plunged into the first chapter of his history.

The old warrior appears to have written slowly and pains-takingly, a few pages at a time, and sometimes for weeks and months he would not touch the manuscript, for there were other things more important than his writing, and a man as active as he found it a chore to stay seated any length of time. He had to supervise his farms, watch over his Indians, see to it that he received his proper income, and as a *regidor* of the city he was often busy attending sessions of the *cabildo*.

This was a period of considerable activity and transition for the province of Guatemala. Rodríguez de Quesada had been ap-pointed as the new president of the *Audiencia* on November 17, 1553, but did not arrive in Guatemala to be sworn in until the early part of 1555.

Among the new *oidores* (members of the *Audiencia*) who took office at the same time was *Licenciado* Alonso de Zorita, with whom Bernal Díaz was friendly. Zorita was an attorney and the *"licenciado"* indicated he had the license to practice law. He also was not a man who took for granted what the colonists and friars told him about the affairs of the province and the conditions of the natives. He wanted to see it all firsthand.

For six months Zorita traveled on foot through the most rugged parts of the country, talking to colonists and Indians and attempting to correct abuses, as well as gathering material for his report. Since this report attacked the treatment of the natives, he soon brought upon himself the hostility of the colonists, who determined to force him out of his official position and out of the province.

Nevertheless, Bernal found that Zorita was often fair and cer-tainly incorruptible at a time when most government officials were interested only in enriching themselves. Bernal thought enough of Zorita to consult him, and as far as we know, he was the first man outside Bernal's family and closest friends to read the beginning of the Díaz manuscript. It is through *Licenciado* Zorita that we learn that Bernal had already begun his account of the Conquest and that he was not in his eighties when he started, as some historians have assumed. Zorita tells about it in his *Historia de la Nueva España:*

> Bernal Díaz del Castillo, citizen of Guatemala, where he has a good *encomienda,* and was a conquistador in that country and in New Spain and in Coatzacoalcos, told me when I was an *oidor* in the *Real Audiencia de los Confines* in the city of Santiago, Guatemala [between 1553 and 1557], that he was writing a history of that country. He showed me part of what he had written. I do not know whether he finished it or whether it has been published.[6]

At the time Bernal Díaz brought the manuscript to Zorita, there were at most sixteen completed chapters. Zorita does not say what he thought of it or whether he encouraged Bernal to go on with it. Bernal possessed little rhetorical style, he had no sense of punctuation, and he was not even a good speller. The learned Zorita was probably more surprised than impressed that a conqueror such as Bernal Díaz, accustomed to the sword, should be devoting himself to preparing a history.

Whatever were Zorita's reactions to Bernal's writings, the rough draft was put away and neglected for some years. Bernal had no inkling at the time that across the sea in Spain, Cortés' chaplain, Francisco López de Gómara, had written a comprehensive story of the Conquest which had already been published

---

[6] Alonso de Zorita, *Historia de la Nueva España,* 23.

and was widely circulated. Copies of it had not yet come to Guatemala.

During the next few years, Bernal Díaz was occupied with his own problems and the affairs of the province. He was at this time also concerned and disgusted over the corrupt politicians the Spanish court sent to Guatemala. He continued to feel that the older settlers like himself, who had served the king well, were not being fairly treated. Important positions of responsibility were given to men new to the country and who lacked knowledge and experience.

Perhaps to forget some of these injustices, Bernal Díaz again turned to the manuscript he had so long neglected. The years were moving fast upon him; if he was ever going to finish it, he knew he must do it soon. He owed it to himself and to the men who had fought alongside him. Furthermore, he was convinced that when this account was sent to the king, it would assure his future and that of his family.

Bernal had barely resumed writing when he acquired a copy of Francisco López de Gómara's *Crónica de la Nueva España*.[7] As he thumbed the pages and began to read, he must have realized that the work to which he was planning to devote the rest of his years had been done by someone else—a priest, a man who had never taken part in the conquest of Mexico or even set foot in the New World. The old warrior glanced at his own manuscript on the desk, at the crude phrases which had come from his pen, then slowly put it away, quite certain he would not touch it again.

We know Bernal Díaz' reaction on reading Gómara's history

[7] This book was first published in Zaragoza in 1552, with a second edition from Medina del Campo in 1553 and still another in 1554. Probably either of the first two was the one Díaz read.

for the first time because he is very precise in describing how he felt about it. The chapters in Bernal's own work are short, and although he had written seventeen of them when he saw Gómara's book, he had barely begun his story and had not even touched upon the Cortés expedition. It was enough to make him abandon his entire project, and he almost did. He did not return to his manuscript merely to combat the errors in Gómara, as some have implied; rather, he wrote his *crónica* notwithstanding the fact that Gómara had beaten him to it, and it is fortunate for literature and history that he did.

Gómara's work was not the only book telling of the Conquest that fell into Bernal's hands. He says he also read the chronicles of Paolo Giovio and Gonzalo de Illescas at this period, though it is not clear how he could have done so. Both these accounts were in Latin, which Bernal admits he could not read, and since Illescas was not put into Spanish until 1564 and Giovio not until 1566, these editions could hardly have reached him in Guatemala so soon after publication in Spain. Either someone read him translated excerpts from these works, for they had been published in Latin long before, or he read translations much later and inserted these names when he was revising his manuscript.

The work which disturbed and irritated him, however, was Gómara's. As he read this well-written history, Bernal realized his own literary limitations. This man Gómara was a priest, a student, and a scholar of prestige; he, Bernal Díaz, was an old soldier, inexperienced in letters and with just enough education to be able to read and write. How could he have dared to try to do what Gómara had done, even if he was a participant and an eyewitness?

Then, as he read on, he began to discover errors, not important ones, but errors nevertheless, in Gómara's story. These were the same sort of mistakes Bernal might well have made and later did make, but they were like barbs in his flesh.

We can well understand Bernal Díaz' envy and anger. Gómara had not shared in the suffering, the anguish, and the defeats that had marked the Conquest. Therefore, Bernal was convinced, Gómara had no right to tell the story of what had been achieved. Furthermore, Gómara gave all the credit to Cortés and "none to us, the true conquerors." Bernal was puzzled by this deliberate snub and then amazed to find that Gómara's work was not dedicated to the king, but to the son of Cortés. Why had Gómara done this?

Bernal slowly began to see the light. Gómara was chaplain to Cortés in the later years in Spain. Cortés provided him with his letters and all the details. Cortés was his main source of information and the book was intended to emphasize the heroic achievements of Cortés. He, Cortés, says Bernal, must have greased the palm of this holy man of letters. There could be no other answer to it:

> When I was writing this my chronicle, by accident I saw what Gómara and Giovio had written about the Conquest of Mexico and New Spain, and when I read them and perceived the elegance of their style, I compared them with my poor efforts and my own vulgar words which were without style or ornament; in view of such fine histories that were in my hands, I decided to abandon my own writing.
>
> With this thought, I started to read those works more thoroughly and to study them, and soon I realized they did not speak of what actually happened in New Spain. They did not even know the size of some of the cities and the number of their inhabitants, and they just as readily put eighty thousand as eight thousand . . . even if the Indians were cowards, we could not have killed as many as

13

they state. . . . They praise some captains and belittle others, and some are mentioned who were not even in the Conquest, and they say so many things which are inaccurate that I will not even point them out.

But what is worse, they say that Cortés sent secretly to destroy the ships and this is not true, because it was done on the advice of all the other soldiers. In all they write very viciously, but why should I waste any more ink and paper in telling about it? And I curse him [Gómara] because he has such an excellent style.

But let us leave this talk and return to the fact that when I had carefully examined what they had written about the occurences in New Spain, I decided to proceed with my own history as it was my plan to tell the truth honestly and without elaborating upon it. . . . I will, therefore, resume, with pen in hand, as a good pilot searching for shoals in the sea ahead, when he knows they will be met with; and this I will do in speaking of the errors of historians, but I shall not mention them all, for if one had to follow item by item, the trouble of discarding the rubbish would be greater than that of gathering the harvest. . . . We know that the truth is something holy and sacred . . . .[8]

Besides those he himself gives, there were several other reasons why Bernal Díaz finally determined to continue the work he had started earlier. One of them was the fact that he had always felt that Cortés had let his men down by never once mentioning them in his letters to the king. Gómara, following Cortés' example, also overlooked the deeds of the common soldier, and the absence of such credit incensed Bernal. He was convinced that no contemporary historian would ever go to the trouble, unless he himself did.

Bernal now made it his job, his mission in life, to take upon his shoulders the work of telling the world that the conquest of

[8] BDC, *cap*. xviii.

Mexico was not a one-man undertaking but a remarkable military achievement for which every soldier was as much responsible as the captains. He was sure that he and his companions had been deliberately pushed into the background and that because of it, none of them had received the rewards they deserved from the king. He knew that the task of coming to their defense as well as his own was up to him, for he was one of the last eyewitnesses left—only five of his companions were still alive. If he, Bernal Díaz, did not do it, the story would forever remain unwritten. He must write a record that could never leave in doubt the part the soldiers had taken in conquering and settling these lands. He did not call his work a memoir, or just a plain history of the Conquest; he named it *historia verdadera,* a true history.

The manuscript was not published while he lived. Even after he was eighty-four, he kept working on it, rewriting and making changes. Today, four hundred years later, his *True History* continues to grow in importance as a dramatic eyewitness account and as a work of literature.

Bernal Díaz said he left his manuscript as a legacy to his family: "I have no other riches to leave my children, but this my true story." But he left it as a legacy to the world, and because of it, we know exactly how the conquest of a new continent was carried out and the type of men who achieved it.

2 ❦ *WHERE WERE THE GOLD AND THE TREASURES?*

B**ERNAL** D**ÍAZ** **DEL** C**ASTILLO** could not have chosen a better time to be born. Spain, after years of subjugation by the Moors, was on the threshold of a new era. The last of the infidel invaders had been driven from Granada and Columbus was already on his second voyage of discovery. In every village, city, and town, from the rolling plains of Andalusia to the mountains of Asturias, the talk was of adventure, of land beyond the ocean sea, and of gold and great treasure. The year was 1496 and the scene of Bernal's birth was the prosperous and important city of Medina del Campo.[1]

---

[1] Genaro García, in his 1904 edition of Bernal Díaz (I, 4), states that Bernal was born in 1492, since Bernal says that he was twenty-four when he was in Cuba. But Bernal was in and out of Cuba for a sufficient number of years to make this extremely vague. More consistent and in agreement are the ages which he later gave when acting as witness to various *probanzas*. These notices would place his birth at 1496. See the note by Joaquín Pardo in Cabañas, III, 3.

He was the son of Francisco Díaz del Castillo and María Díaz de Rejón.[2] His father was a *regidor* of Medina del Campo and the family of some prominence. Of himself and his comrades Bernal wrote:

> We were most of us *hidalgos,* although not all of such clear lineage because in this world, all men are not born equal, either in generosity or in virtue. . . . But whatever may have been our backgrounds we made ourselves much more illustrious by our heroic actions in the conquest.[3]

If Bernal Díaz came from a large family, he failed to say so. He speaks merely of an older brother who found work in the government. Both brothers went to school and learned to read and write. While in the past education had been limited to people of means and the clergy, there was now throughout Spain an awakening to learning. Books were being published in large quantities and the market was flooded with science-fiction type stories that did not lack imagination in describing the New

[2] Bernal Díaz never mentions his mother's name, essentially because Spanish usage of the day did not require it. Yet his children knew her name, for we find that his great-great-grandson, Antonio Francisco Fuentes y Guzmán, called her María Díaz de Rejón. The best sources for this type of information are baptismal registers and records, but those which have been examined in the four parish churches of Medina del Campo go back only to mid–fifteenth century. However, the *libro de acuerdos* for the year 1490, still extant in the city's *ayuntamiento,* lists among municipal officers one Diego del Castillo, who was probably the father of Francisco Díaz del Castillo, since the office of *regidor* was often hereditary. There were *regidores* with the surnames Díaz and Díez del Castillo throughout the sixteenth century in Medina del Campo.

[3] BDC, *cap.* ccvii.

17

World. As boys of today dream of spaceships and trips to the moon, so in Bernal Díaz' time they dreamed of adventure and of the riches which might be found in the land Columbus had discovered.[4]

Spanish settlements had already been established in Cuba, Jamaica, and La Isla Española (now Haiti and the Dominican Republic), and every month new expeditions were being equipped and sent to these lands of mystery and untold wealth. It was an exciting and glorious period in which to be young. Bernal knew it, and not much deliberation was needed on his part to reach a decision on what he would do. Because of his father's position, he might have followed his brother's example and taken a government job. But who wants office work when there is a chance of becoming a conqueror?

As Bernal grew into a lad of fifteen, his mind was made up. He would leave his home when the best opportunity presented itself. Apparently neither his father nor his mother approved of his plans, for if they had, with his father's influence, Bernal would not have gone off as an ordinary soldier. There must have been a definite break with his parents which he preferred not to remember.

An older man alone with his memories often thinks of his youth. Yet as Bernal Díaz, ordinarily quite garrulous, never forgetting the smallest detail, set out to write the story of the Conquest, he skipped every mention of his early years. There is also no indication that he wrote to his family in Spain and no hint of his longing to return to the country of his birth. Other conquerors spoke of the wealth they would take home. Not Díaz. He never looked back.

[4] See Irving Leonard, *Books of the Brave,* for illuminating discussion of the intellectual aspects of the Conquest.

A MONG THE MAYAS, the Aztecs, and the Tlascalans were artists who recorded important events. Many of their drawings and paintings made just before and during the Conquest are still extant in various museum collections. Among the most descriptive are those known as the *Lienzo de Tlaxcala,* reproduced here by courtesy of the Bancroft Library. They are taken from *Mexico: Junta Colombina, Homenaje á Cristóbal Colón, Antigüedades Mexicanas, Mexico, Oficina Tipográfico de la Secretaria de Fomento, 1892 Atlas.*

Yepotlpan. Eoncáqnamicqsmtlatoque qmacaqyxqdqqualom.

Aztec Gifts for Cortés

When Montezuma learned of the Cortés expedition's arrival in Veracruz, he sent messengers bearing gifts of jade, gold, and food. This
painting depicts Cortés, accompanied by his native consort and interpreter, Malinche, receiving the royal gifts. Behind them stand Spanish
soldiers and some of the Spaniards' native allies.

CHRISTIANITY COMES TO NEW SPAIN

The Spaniards were deeply religious and looked upon the Conquest as an opportunity to bring Christianity to the natives of these new lands. Here Cortés greets a Tlascalan chief who is embracing the Cross.

vitzilapan.

THE DEFEAT AND CAPTURE OF NARVÁEZ

Cortés left Cuba without obtaining official sanction for his expedition. Soon after the conquest of Mexico was under way, he was confronted with an enemy as formidable as the native warriors: a large group of Spanish soldiers, led by Pánfilo Narváez, who had instructions to arrest Cortés. For a time it was a battle between Spaniards, and then Cortés quickly defeated Narváez. In this painting the Tlascalan artists depict, at upper left, the defeat of Narváez' army. At lower left, Cortés puts Narváez in irons.

tepeyacac.

CORTÉS AT TEPEACA

Bernal Díaz describes in his story of the Conquest the many battles the Spaniards fought en route to Mexico City. One of the most important was at Tepeaca, in what is now Puebla. Here Cortés and his Indian allies are seen vanquishing the defenders, whose arms consist of *chimalli* (shields) and *macanas* (obsidian-edged war clubs). One of the invading Indians is disguised as an animal.

THE BATTLE OF METZTITLÁN

In Nahuatl, the word *Metztitlán* means "Place of the Moon" (see figure at upper right). Shown here is another hard-fought battle in which the Cortés expedition was engaged. The Spaniards, says Bernal Díaz, preferred death in battle to capture, for they knew that as prisoners they would be tortured and eventually sacrificed to the native gods.

CORTÉS MEETS MONTEZUMA

This painting describes Cortés' arrival in Mexico City, or Tenochtitlán, on November 8, 1519. Montezuma is seated facing Cortés and the ever present Malinche, interpreter to the two principals. The Aztec chiefs, it is interesting to note, are not dressed in Aztec robes; instead, the Tlascalan artists have painted them in Tlascalan attire.

THE SPANIARDS FLEE MEXICO CITY

On *La Noche Triste* ("The Sad Night"), the Aztecs turned against the
Spaniards and forced them out of Mexico City. In this scene the Tlascalan
artists show Cortés and his men fighting their way out under the protection of wooden "tanks."

ALVARADO AT QUEZALTENANGO

Soon after the conquest of Mexico, the Spaniards began to explore and take possession of other areas, including what is now the state of Chiapas. One of Cortés' principal lieutenants was Pedro de Alvarado, whom Bernal Díaz admired. Known as "The Conqueror of Guatemala," Alvarado is here shown in battle at Quezaltenango.

When he finally joined the expedition which took him first to Darién and then to Cuba, Bernal broke all ties with the Old World and his family. He was a young soldier of some education and ability among a group that included hardened adventurers. If things at home had been easier, his father would have provided him with the means to be well equipped with the necessary armor and a good horse. Instead, he went out as a common foot soldier, and later, for only a few short weeks, he held the rank of an officer.

There are portraits of Bernal Díaz, but like those of Columbus, Pedro de Alvarado, and others, they were painted years after death. We have only a vague idea of what Bernal looked like in his youth or in later life; we can merely surmise from what he himself wrote, what his friends said of him, and from other evidence which may or may not be reliable.[5]

He writes of his father's being known as *el galán,* the handsome one. Much later he relates that among the troops of Sandoval there were three soldiers named Castillo and that to differentiate them, one was called Castillo the thinker, another, the thoughtful one, and the third, Castillo *el galán.* The handsome one, Bernal admits without modesty, was himself.

[5] The painting of Bernal Díaz in La Casa de Popenoe in Antigua and the one reproduced in various editions of his work are of dubious origin. Edward O. Heinrich, a handwriting expert who studied the Bernal Díaz manuscript, gave me a hypothetical description of Bernal Díaz:

> Bernal Díaz was evidently a man who lived heartily, with vigor and gusto. If you cover that part of his signature which follows the "B," you will discover that he has given us a self-portrait. In my opinion he had a high forehead, rather close-set eyes, a Cyrano de Bergerac nose and an attentive ear. Bernal was an observant man, inclined to be a bit suspicious, but fully confident of his own power to overcome opposition. Subconsciously he crossed himself before writing his signature and the cross observance was woven into his "B."

In 1539, when witnesses were asked if Bernal Díaz had much fame as a conversationalist, each testified that this was true and that he liked to live well and was known for his honesty and integrity. On the two occasions he went to Spain, he was certainly listened to, for each time he returned with royal orders granting him special favors and compensations. But he lacked the diplomacy and the smoothness of Cortés, even when he addressed letters to the king. Bernal felt, as did many of his fellow conquerors, that he had not been treated as he deserved and had the right to expect.

At times he was an opportunist, but he was intelligent and sharp in his observations, and he had the ability to grasp new languages and new ideas quickly. In the three years he was in Cuba, he learned the native dialect, and while in Mexico he probably spoke Nahuatl and much later the Cakchiquel language of the Guatemalan Indians. He also had some firm convictions on how the country should be governed and was not backward in expressing them. But he had no sense for business; he acquired very little wealth and usually lived beyond his means.

Bernal Díaz was just eighteen when, in 1514, he left his home in Medina del Campo and rode through the Spanish countryside on his way toward the city of Seville. He arrived in time to sign on as a volunteer in the expedition of Pedrarias Dávila.[6] Dávila staged an impressive review in the plaza and marched his soldiers—Bernal Díaz among them—past the cathedral and across the famous Puente de Triana to the fleet waiting in the river.

[6] Henry Raup Wagner, "Three Studies on the Same Subject," *Hispanic*

As the townspeople cried out *"buen viaje, buena suerte,"* the ships began to move slowly down the Río de Guadalquivir. The crowds on the banks and on the stone bridge grew smaller; now all Bernal Díaz and his companions could make out was the high tower of the cathedral, silhouetted against the blue Spanish sky. Soon the fleet reached the port of Sanlúcar de Barrameda, and from there it sailed out of the Gulf of Cádiz on a course west by north.

Bernal Díaz had joined the expedition as a soldier, and he had little, if any, contact with the officers or the members of the rich entourage of the new governor. But he was not the only future historian or conqueror aboard. On this same voyage were Pascual de Andagoya, who later described the trip, and Gonzalo Fernández de Oviedo y Valdés, who, as an official historian, was later to write many volumes on the Indies. Others who went along included Hernando de Soto, the discoverer of the Mississippi, Sebastián de Belalcázar, the conqueror of Ecuador, and Diego de Almagro, who was to share with Pizarro the honors of vanquishing the Incas of Peru.

After leaving Spain the ships put in at various islands to cap-

American Historical Review, Vol. XXV (1945), 155–211. In what is otherwise an excellent summary of Bernal Díaz' early activities in the Indies, Mr. Wagner accuses Bernal of faking his claim that he came out with Pedrarias in 1514 and goes on to deny that Bernal went on the Yucatán voyage of 1518. I find Mr. Wagner's deductions to be based upon hypothetical rather than documentary evidence. One Spanish authority, Bermúdez Plata, in a letter to me, disagrees with Mr. Wagner's observations. "I cannot find evidence to reach such a conclusion," he states. And professor Lesley Byrd Simpson of the University of California, who has done considerable research on Bernal Díaz, writes me: "If you have to choose between Wagner and Bernal Díaz about the Pedrarias expedition, you will do well to follow the latter. After all, he was in a somewhat better position to know and I see no possible motive for his faking it. . . . I should certainly go along with Bermúdez Plata."

ture Caribs for slaves, then continued to Darién, where they arrived on June 20, some two months later.

Hunger and disease went together in this marshy, unhealthy country. From twenty to thirty persons died daily, and often the great holes in which the dead were cast were not covered because there were always more bodies to be buried. This was far from the glamorous New World which Bernal Díaz and the rest had envisioned, so, he says, "some of us gentlemen and persons of quality asked and were granted permission to depart for the island of Cuba." But he was putting it mildly, for what many of the colonists did was to escape from this hazardous region as fast as they could. In the few ships still remaining in port, one group of colonists sailed for Spain, another for La Isla Española, and the others to Cuba. Bernal Díaz was in this last boatload.

Exactly what he did, how he lived during the three years he was in Cuba, Bernal chooses not to recall, but obviously he did not prosper. He later admitted that he was forced to accept clothing from a friend from his home town of Medina del Campo. "In my poverty," he wrote, "I had only the willingness to work left."

Where were the gold and the treasures? Where was all the wealth he had overheard talk about in the *mesónes* in Spain? Here were only a hot climate, disease, and misery. Bernal was young and ambitious and he must have felt that he was fated for better luck than this. If wealth was ever to be in his path, he knew he had to look for it.

Others on the island were of the same opinion, including many who had traveled with him from Darién. They were convinced that the only way to find a fortune was to search for and explore new lands. But this took money and a leader. An expedition was an expensive operation, and they had no money and little like-

Map by Antonio Sotomayor

CORTÉS' ROUTE FROM VERACRUZ TO MEXICO CITY (TENOCHTITLÁN)

lihood of getting any. They talked, listened, and argued, and just as they were about to abandon hope of leaving Cuba, word reached them that Francisco de Córdoba, a Spaniard of wealth and position, was organizing an expedition. Bernal says they chose Córdoba as their leader, but the chances are he selected them and they gladly accepted.

The expedition of Columbus to discover the route to the Indies was eventually financed by the Spanish crown. Columbus spent years attempting to get financial support. In the expeditions of Córdoba and Cortés, however, they did not ask or depend upon a government subsidy. From their own money they purchased ships and equipped them, hoping, of course, that the gold they would find would more than compensate them for their expenses

and efforts. Nevertheless, the Spanish crown always had a representative on these expeditions to make certain the royal fifth
was collected.

It was Córdoba's money which was used to purchase the ships
for the expedition and to buy cordage, anchors, wooden casks
to hold water, and all the other necessary equipment. None
of it was easy to find in Cuba, but somehow they managed to
locate what they needed.

Their next problem was to provide food for the voyage. Since
there were few domestic animals in Cuba at the time, their
meat supply consisted of bacon and live pigs, which, Bernal Díaz
painstakingly recalled, cost three pesos each. Bread made of
native cassava root was included, plus salt, chick-peas, lentils,
and beans. Olive oil in huge earthenware jars from Spain was
brought aboard, and there were enough *botijas* of wine to provide at least a glassful for each meal.

They had luck in finding good pilots, for one of them was
Antonio de Alaminos, who had been chief pilot on Columbus'
last voyage and on Ponce de León's expedition to Florida. In
order that everything should proceed on the "right principles,"
they took a priest and a representative of the king, "so that if
God willed that we should come on rich lands, or people who
possess gold or silver or pearls or any other things of treasure,
there should be a responsible person to guard the Royal Fifth,"
or what amounted to the king's share of the spoils—one-fifth
of everything.

On February 8, 1517, the three ships, with a strong wind filling
their sails, set out on a southwest course. Bernal Díaz and his
one hundred shipmates were on their way to becoming conquerors.

26

3   "MANY OF US FELT AS IF WE WERE DREAMING"

In the space of the next few years, Bernal Díaz led a dramatic and exciting life. He killed natives in battle and he was wounded. He accompanied expeditions which discovered Yucatán Peninsula and, what they were later to realize, an entire new continent.

These early expeditions in which Bernal Díaz participated, important as they were, did not result in the establishment of any colonies or in finding gold and other riches. They did, however, raise the curtain for the biggest drama and the greatest achievement of all: the conquest of Mexico.

The story of how Cortés and his small army vanquished the Aztecs and destroyed their empire has been described many times. Bernal Díaz took part throughout the campaign, from the start to the end. It was the most important episode in his life.

While that event perhaps rightfully belongs in a biography of Bernal Díaz, even a brief account of it is far too lengthy to be included within the scope of this work.[1] Bernal Díaz tells it

[1] The best short account of the Conquest in English is to be found in

graphically and dramatically, and the reader is referred to the best authoritative work on the subject, Bernal Díaz' own *True History of the Conquest of Mexico*.

We are at the moment more interested in the man and his companions than the Conquest. Yet we will touch on certain phases of it because they tell us a good deal about Bernal Díaz.

I shall later describe the expedition to Honduras, in which Bernal participated, because in narrating it we get to know him better. In the conquest of Mexico, however, Hernán Cortés was the principal actor; Bernal Díaz played a minor role, though it was the soldiers such as he who made the Conquest possible.

If in the beginning the natives believed the Spaniards to be gods, they soon realized there was nothing omnipotent about men who sustained wounds, became ill, and died. Although Montezuma believed in some respects the legend of Quetzalcóatl and that bearded white gods would return to his country, he was too intelligent to accept the Spaniards as anything but human beings. "The Tlascalans, I know, have informed thee that I am like a god and that my houses are all of gold, silver and precious stones," he said to Cortés. "But now thou see it that I am of flesh and blood as thou art and that my houses are of lime, stone and timber. These ridiculous falsehoods about me, thou hast treated them with the same contempt as I do the stories I have been told of thee producing thunder and lightning."[2]

Nonetheless, there was something about the Spaniards, with their heavy armor, their steel swords glistening in the sun, their horses champing at the bits, the guns that blasted with fire, and

F. A. Kirkpatrick, *The Spanish Conquistadores*. The classic full account is William H. Prescott's *History of the Conquest of Mexico*, in many editions.

[2] BDC, *cap.* xc.

the cannon which shook the ground, to create a sense of fear in all those who came in contact with them.

Soon what fears they might have had left them. Yet they knew they had no steel armor to protect themselves as had the Spaniards and that their weapons were no match against the guns and the sharp swords of the enemy which had invaded their country. The Mexicans, however, far outnumbered the forces of Cortés, and they could easily have turned the Spaniards back if Montezuma had given the word. But Montezuma, timid, superstitious and half-believing the legend he had heard from childhood that Quetzalcóatl would return to rule over his people, failed to act in time.

Cortés took full advantage of the situation. He was a born strategist and planned every move. He had also selected his men with great care, for they had to have tremendous endurance in order to withstand the suffering, hardships, and defeats which marked the Conquest.

They were not ordinary soldiers either. While they sought adventure and riches, they were also convinced they were religious crusaders. They prayed before and after every battle, and the Cross was as important as the sword. Bernal Díaz and soldiers like himself, wearing armor and on horses, might have looked formidable to the Mexicans, yet the Spaniards were small in stature. Bashford Dean, who has measured many suits of fifteenth-century armor at the Metropolitan Museum in New York, believes that their wearers were much smaller and leaner than men today. Dr. T. D. Stewart of the Smithsonian Institution points out that even now "the Spanish in general are among the shortest European group."[3]

[3] Bashford Dean, *Handbook of Arms and Armor,* chap. X. The quote from Dr. Stewart is taken from a letter to me.

Certainly in height they did not tower over their Mexican foes. Paintings in codices of the Aztecs show the Spaniards of about the same stature as the Mexicans. The Spaniards look heavier and stronger than the natives, but this was due to their armor. Bernal Díaz writes that he himself was of average height: "I am as tall as the generality of men."

Was a conqueror of New Spain proportionately stronger than a young officer today? Dean, from the studies he has conducted, concludes that "he could do in his armor what few modern athletes could do without special training. And we are convinced," he adds, "that he stood the strain longer and under greater mental and physical stress, but only on account of his experience."[4]

The Spaniards were not too heavily weighted down with armor, which usually covered only from the trunk up. Their legs were free and unprotected, except for long stockings and high boots of soft leather. They wore their armor constantly, and Bernal Díaz writes that throughout the march to the capital and until the Aztecs were defeated, he always went to bed fully dressed for battle, with his weapons by his side.

They did carry themselves as gods and conquerors, and they looked the part. For one thing, most of them were comparatively young men. Cortés, as captain-general, was barely thirty-four; Gonzalo de Sandoval, one of his closest lieutenants, twenty-two; Pedro de Alvarado, twenty-four; and Bernal Díaz, twenty-three. There were some oldsters—several of whom had been in military campaigns in Italy—but most of the men were under thirty. Many of the older ones died on the way, others during the early days of the Conquest.

[4] Dean, *op. cit.,* 239. See also Herbert Cerwin, *These Are the Mexicans,* 167, on the effects of Mexico City's altitude.

It had to be a young army. Only youth could have endured the long marches, often on empty stomachs, the strange foods they had to eat when they did eat, the lack of sanitation, the tropical fevers, and the changing climate as they passed from *tierra caliente* of the lowlands to *tierra fría* on the Mexican Plateau. Yet Bernal Díaz rarely complained of the severe weather and "the cutting winds of the Sierra Nevada which made us shiver." He never mentions the 7,400-foot altitude, which must have taxed their strength and energy. Such was their stamina that they thought nothing of climbing across those long ranges of mountains or even of ascending the highest volcano.

When Montezuma suggested to Cortés that he should be carried or helped down the steps of the great Temple of Huitzil-opochtli, as he must be tired, Cortés responded that fatigue was unknown to them. But Bernal admits that descending the 114 steps of the temple was not done so easily: "Particularly those of our soldiers who were suffering from *bubas* found that the going down was painful."[5]

The conquerors had only the most rudimentary knowledge of sanitation and medicine. In these two respects the Aztecs, with their steam baths and medicinal herbs (some of which are still used in modern pharmacology), were far advanced compared to sixteenth-century Europeans.[6] In one of his letters to the king, Cortés praised the skill of the native doctors who had attended him and his men and indicated that for the moment the sending of Spanish physicians was not necessary.

With the possible exception of syphilis, or what the Spaniards called *bubas,* the natives were free of most of the diseases common

[5] BDC, *cap.* xcii.

[6] See Bernardino de Sahagún, *Historia general de las cosas de Nueva España,* II, 416.

in the Old World. Malaria, smallpox, yellow fever, and even tuberculosis, all of which later took a tremendous toll in lives, were unknown to them.[7] Some authorities believe that there were no rats or mice prior to the Conquest, but recent excavations of Maya tombs in Uaxactún, Guatemala, definitely prove their existence, although typhus was probably not prevalent.

Had any of these diseases existed among the natives at the time the Spaniards landed at Veracruz, they perhaps would never have reached the Mexican capital. Sickness was not a serious problem at first, though the men did suffer from fevers of unknown origin and from dysentery, the latter frequently caused by the kind of food they ate. The surgeon whom Cortés brought along was of little help. For their own wounds, Bernal maintains that he and his companions usually depended on a salve made from the fat of Indians killed in battle.

When provisions were plentiful, the conquerors ate corn, beans, chilies, native fruits, turkeys, fowl, and meats from wild animals, but when they were among unfriendly natives and in the midst of battles, their rations were slim. Many times these lusty Spaniards were entirely without food, and when hunger gnawed at their insides, they were forced to eat whatever they found. "Sometimes," Bernal wrote, "the dogs we caught afforded us a good supper."

Once in a while they washed their undergarments in the rivers, but the soldiers who bathed were rare; Europeans of that period usually shied from it. Compared to the Spaniards, the

---

[7] One authority, Sylvanus G. Morley, dismisses the theory that yellow fever and malaria decimated the Mayan empire "for the simple reason that neither malaria nor yellow fever was prevalent in the Americas before the coming of the white man." *The Ancient Maya,* 69. See also P. M. Ashburn, *The Ranks of Death: A Medical History of the Conquest.*

Aztecs were fastidious, for they bathed regularly in steam baths and shampooed their hair with the pulp of avocados, as many native women do to this day. The Spaniards may have had the appearance of gods, but to the Indians they smelled bad.

Bernal Díaz frequently refers to natives who swung incense burners of copal as the Spaniards approached. He believed this was done out of respect and in tribute to them. The historian Artemio de Valle-Arizpe, however, advances the conjecture that the burning of incense by the Aztecs was done not out of reverence "but because they could not stand the strong smells of the Spaniards which came from the sweat that had gathered on their bodies, for they never bathed. How they must have stunk, not only from sweat but from dried blood and unhealed wounds!"[8]

Originally, Bernal was critical of his general, but he never failed to recognize the leadership of Cortés and the hold he had on his men. "There never was a captain in the world," he said, "who was better obeyed." Fifty years after the Conquest, as he recalled the actions of his commander, his pen dripped with praise of Cortés.

While it is true that Cortés' own private fortune stood behind the enterprise, he was vain, selfish, and greedy for loot: he was going to get all he could for Hernán Cortés. A little tolerance and generosity on his part would have done much to prevent the constant friction between him and his men, and he would have been a far greater man if he had given more credit to his soldiers and officers for their accomplishments. Despite his loyalty to Cortés, Bernal Díaz felt this neglect keenly.

It was more than Cortés' qualities of leadership or his disciplinary measures which kept the army together. Although

[8] *Andanzas de Hernán Cortés,* 64.

33

Bernal Díaz had a realistic approach toward religion and did not believe in miracles, his own fears and those of his companions drove them to a faith that was overpowering. Without this faith, without the sincere and almost fanatic belief that it was their mission to bring Christianity to the natives, they might have failed. From it they gained their strength, their will to go on, when everything seemed lost. "Above all was the great mercy of God who gave us force to sustain their attacks," Bernal often reminds us. The Spaniards were carrying not only the flag of their king and country but the white banner of God as well.

While Bernal Díaz was in a sense deeply religious and critical of certain priests who had committed wrongs as men, he never criticized them as representatives of the Church. He said his prayers regularly before and after battles, and he rarely faced the enemy without recommending himself to God and the Holy Virgin and invoking the aid of Santiago. "We prepared for battle," he wrote, "by confessing to our reverend fathers, who were occupied during the whole night in that holy office."

If the Spaniards succeeded and their lives were preserved, it was because of their trust in God; if they failed, it was the will of God. If they sinned, it was only when necessary; God provided and God would forgive. Bernal himself never removed the silver medallion of the Virgin which he wore on a chain around his neck; he was still wearing it when he was buried.

With such a man as Cortés as its leader and with God on its side, the little army of about four hundred men was formidable. Thus in the month of August, 1519, Bernal Díaz and his fellow soldiers received the order to march, across valleys made green by heavy rains and over the narrow trails of the mountain ranges, toward the Aztec capital. Less than a month before, the thought of entering the Mexican stronghold had been treated by Bernal as something of a joke. "It made some of us laugh to think we should try to make the attempt," he wrote.

As they descended through a mountain range, Bernal Díaz caught his first glimpse of the Mexican capital. He had not anticipated a city which in beauty and simplicity rivaled the cities of Spain.

He saw now an oval island connected with the mainland by three causeways, pierced by bridges, which converged at the center of the city. The edges of the island were fringed by the green of the "floating gardens," and toward its center the shiny white of rooftops predominated, the green being reduced to the little squares of patio gardens. Thrust above the quadrate mass of the rooftops loomed the various temples, each set on its pyramid. There were few streets or open spaces in the city, which was gridded with canals crossed by drawbridges.

"We stood there admiring what we saw, and we said it all appeared to us like the enchanted things we had read in the book of Amadis," Bernal wrote. "There were great towers and temples and other edifices of lime and stone which were constructed along the avenues of water. Many of us felt as if we were dreaming it and some may question the manner in which I express myself, for never did man hear, see or vision of what we saw on that day."[9]

Yet when many years later Bernal Díaz sat down at his desk, faced the long sheets of *papel de barba,* and tried to remember what happened on that eventful November day in 1519, he was awed by his very memory. Had it really been that way? Did not the years and his eyes deceive him? If he had only kept a notebook or a written record, he could be more positive. He must not lie, he must not elaborate too much; there were other conquerors

[9] BDC, *cap.* lxxxvii.

still alive who could refute what he had to say. "But all which I witnessed," he wrote, "gradually came back to me as if it all had occurred yesterday. For this I give thanks to Our Lord Jesus Christ, for having guarded me through all the dangers and perils and then permitting me to write in my humble way of what I took part in and saw."

The strange city, with its terraced houses, its towering temples, and its canals, proved fascinating to Bernal Díaz; he had never seen anything like it. All along the causeway were native warriors, their bodies covered with vests of quilted cotton so thick that arrows could not penetrate yet so light and serviceable that the Spaniards would soon adopt them to replace their heavier armor. The wealthier chieftains and nobles were wearing *tilmahtli,* cloaks made of cotton or featherwork, thrown over their shoulders and tied at the neck; around their loins they had sashes, richly embroidered and ornamented with fringe or tassels. The native women were elegantly attired for the occasion in colorful skirts with decorated borders and loose cotton blouses with hand-woven designs. They wore thick necklaces of gold and jade and long earrings to match. Here and there Bernal caught a glimpse of a pretty face and what might be the semblance of a smile, though generally the faces were sullen and expressionless.

The throng of people was so great that Bernal could not count them. They had come from all the neighboring communities to look at these bearded men, these white gods on horses who produced lightning and thunder and feared no one.

Bernal Díaz, a mere stripling of twenty-three, was about to see the mighty Montezuma, was about to witness the groundbreaking for a new world. He was like most youthful soldiers, anxious and excited. He had come a long way for this day and this moment. The suffering, the terror he had witnessed, the

36

wounds he had received, were nothing to the thrill and satisfaction he now felt. He, Bernal Díaz del Castillo, was seeing
what Spain and the rest of the world would soon be talking
about. There was gold to be shared, too, and with gold he could
buy everything he had ever wanted. Perhaps an estate, with
Indians to till the soil and add to his wealth; one or two fine
horses; a house with servants; and of course a wife from a good
family, and children to follow. The king was certain to reward
him with a suitable coat of arms; from now on, he could cease
being a nobody. But he must stop dreaming. The trumpets were
sounding and the drums were rolling. The great Montezuma
was approaching.

After Montezuma was taken as a prisoner by the Spaniards,
it is popularly believed that the Aztec leader was badly treated,
but Bernal Díaz makes a point of stressing that they grew fond
of Montezuma. He says they regarded him with respect and
honor and that he was assigned a Spanish page.

Through the page, Bernal wormed his way into the emperor's good will. "Whenever I was on guard," Bernal says, "and
passed in front of him, I doffed my beret with the greatest respect. The page told him I had come to these lands twice before
Cortés and this seemed to interest him."

Bernal hinted to the page that he would be pleased if Montezuma presented him with a handsome Indian girl of noble birth.
When this request reached the emperor's ears, according to
Bernal, he was summoned before him and he quotes Montezuma
as saying: "They tell me that thou art poor in cloth and gold
and have other desires. So today I am going to present thee with
a pretty maid. Treat her well, as she is the daughter of one of my
principales and her family will give thee gold and mantles."

According to Bernal, he bowed from the waist and, holding
his quilted beret over his heart, said to Montezuma: "For this

37

favor thou hast granted me, I kiss thy royal hands. May Our Lord God prosper thee and preserve thee."

Bernal, who seldom lost an opportunity of putting in a good word for himself, now quoted Montezuma as saying to the page: "It appears to me this Bernal Díaz is a person of excellent qualities."[10]

Even if Montezuma failed to make such an observation, he at least thought enough of the young Spanish guard to present him with three blocks of gold and two loads of mantles. Then later in the day, true to his promise, the emperor produced an Indian maiden for him. She was called Doña Francisca, "a lady of good birth as she showed in her manners."

Bernal Díaz had finally managed to get for himself an Indian woman of rank. How long she remained with him and what became of her, he does not tell us. Later he had an Indian common-law wife, but she was not Doña Francisca. Many years were yet to pass before he would settle down, and when he was finally married by the Church, it was to a young Spanish widow.

[10] *Ibid., cap.* xcvii.

4 🎜 ON THE MARCH AGAIN

THE Spanish army was successful and the great city of Mexico lay in ruins. Bernal Díaz, however, had grave doubts concerning what, in reality, he and his companions had achieved. He was shocked by the destruction. "But of all these wonders which I saw, there is nothing left," he wrote. "If my own eyes had not seen them, I would not believe that what was once a great city is no more."

Bernal Díaz wanted his share of the loot, but he was not too avaricious about it. He had a lusty feeling about life, a great esteem for his comrades, and a certain piety and moral sense which made him sensitive and critical. Bernal might have been a priest instead of a soldier; indeed, three of his children later entered the priesthood, and one of his grandsons became dean of the Cathedral of Guatemala.

There has been much conjecture with regard to why Bernal Díaz, with all his ability and good sense, failed to rise in the ranks of the army. We know him as a historian, but not as the excellent soldier he must have been. Cortés mentioned him in a letter only once, and that was some years after the Conquest and consisted merely of a passing reference that he had served him well. Bernal was not one to turn down favors and rewards which come with being an officer. It seems probable that he would have grasped at the chance, as he did on that one occasion preceding the march to Honduras.[1]

There is one possible explanation of why he was not given a real opportunity to prove himself: at the time of the Conquest, he must have lacked the qualities of leadership. Cortés would not have overlooked Bernal Díaz if he thought him capable of being an officer. But if Bernal did not have the necessary qualifications or was not given the chance to exert them, he nevertheless managed to take good care of himself. In providing for his own needs, he was resourceful and shrewd. Somehow, he invariably managed to have a little wine set aside for his use when others had none; he saw to it that he never went hungry if it was at all possible to make previous arrangements. When there was no wine or water to drink, even Cortés and his captains relied on him. "They each took a drink from the pitcher my servants carried well concealed, for thirst knows no law," Bernal wrote.

This time Bernal had servants, as did some of the other soldiers and officers, for after the Conquest the Spaniards had begun a practice, which lasted for some years, of branding captured Indians as war prisoners and turning them into slaves. Bernal had acquired four of them, not to mention his *indias muy bonitas*.

During the early period of the Conquest, Bernal was an adven-

---

[1] In *cap.* viii of his manuscript, Bernal wrote that he had been named *sargento*, then crossed it out and substituted *alférez*. The latter word is of Arabic origin, and according to the *Enciclopedia Universal Ilustrada de Espasa-Calpe,* there is little difference between the two terms as far as rank is concerned. The *alférez*, however, is always the company standard-bearer.

turous soldier of fortune with no responsibilities besides saving his own skin. Let others do the worrying and the planning, he would follow and do his duty. As a soldier, he proved time and time again that he was no coward, but he had a sincere regard for fear, which he willingly admitted. "Before I entered into battle," he wrote, "I was so frightened, I had to urinate several times, and in my heart I felt great horror; then after committing myself to God and to His Blessed Mother, my terror left me."[2]

To survive the Conquest, Bernal had to be a realist. He could easily condone the slaying of an Indian or the branding of one into slavery, and there was certainly nothing wrong in taking a pretty native maid to bed, but he could not pardon the avarice and brutality his companions displayed after the fall of Mexico City. He was shocked by the excesses of the soldiers and the officers who, while the city was still strewn with the dead, began to celebrate their victory.

At near-by Coyoacán they held a banquet which soon developed into the most drunken debauch Bernal had ever seen. His friends, with whom he had fought, could talk of nothing but gold, of the golden saddles and armor they would have. As the wine took effect, some of the conquerors of New Spain jumped and walked over the tops of the tables, and others came rolling down the steps of the stairway. Bernal wrote it all as he remembered it. Then, much later, perhaps having some twinges of conscience about the malice of his companions, he deleted this incident from his manuscript.

Bernal and most of his fellow soldiers had assumed that when the Aztec capital fell, they would be both conquerors and rich men. They were bitterly disappointed on realizing they had actually gained nothing. Their dreams of gold were gone; they

[2] BDC, *cap.* clvi.

had not enough money to pay for medicines for their wounds and fevers. Many of the soldiers were actually in debt. Some had paid as much as fifty crowns for a crossbow and a thousand crowns for a horse. They owed the surgeons of the expedition, as well as the apothecary and the barber, both of whom Bernal accused of charging excessive rates. The conquerors, who should have been happy over their victory, were disgruntled and embittered. Some scribbled slandering remarks on the white walls of the house Cortés had taken for himself, and others loudly proclaimed that Cortés had reaped all the profits and should be forced to share them.

The graft and corruption which have riddled Mexico and most of Latin America ever since set in soon after the Conquest. As Bernal Díaz reports, some of his companions thought nothing of altering what little gold they had by mixing it with copper. He then goes on to state that the governor sent to replace Cortés was bought off with gold. Although the conquerors were displeased with Cortés, Bernal points out that they came to Cortés' defense when he was accused of having poisoned a representative of the king.[3]

Bernal Díaz soon felt that Mexico City, drained of its treasures, was no place to stay if he was ever going to make his fortune. This opinion was strengthened when he heard that his friend Gonzalo de Sandoval was planning an expedition into the interior of Mexico. He was certain that Sandoval would not set out without good prospects. Bernal quietly began to make inquiries and shortly found that the books which contained the accounts of Montezuma's revenues had been examined to determine which districts the various tributes of gold, cacao, and

[3] *Ibid., cap.* cxciv.

cotton mantles came from and that Sandoval had chosen to explore the region which had sent the largest tributes.

Bernal had no trouble reaching a decision. In the radius of Mexico City, only corn and maguey plants were cultivated; there were no mines, no large plantations, and no cotton for making cloth. Away from the capital the prospects were uncertain, but they at least offered greater reward. Bernal sought out Sandoval, who apparently had a liking for him. He agreed, if permission could be obtained from Cortés. Not losing any time, Bernal went to see Cortés.

Cortés must have smiled inwardly at the optimism of the young soldier who had been with him through so much, for when he answered him, he said: "I think you often deceive yourself. Naturally I prefer that you stay here with me. But if you are determined to go with our friend Sandoval, go by all means. I will always see that you are taken care of, though you will repent this decision you have made."[4]

The expedition of Sandoval had two common objectives. One was to explore the surrounding country for gold; the second, to establish settlements in regions which would prove profitable for farming.

A few outright grants of land were made to the conquerors, but the crown was strict in that no property should be seized from the Indians. Instead, an *encomienda* system was established as a method of providing the Spanish settlers with a certain labor supply. Lesley Byrd Simpson writes of it:

> As developed in the Antilles, the encomienda was at first (up to the passage of the New Laws of 1542) the delegation of the royal

[4] *Ibid., cap.* clvii.

43

power to collect tribute from, and to use the personal services of the King's vassals (the Indians). The encomendero undertook to look after the welfare of his charges and to educate them in proper (Spanish) norms of conduct, as well as to discharge the usual feudal obligation of bearing arms in the King's defense. In reality the encomienda, at least in the first fifty years of its existence, was looked upon by its beneficiaries as a subterfuge for slavery, and it was only after half a century of furious agitation on the part of Las Casas and the reformers, and the active interest of the Crown in suppressing it, that it was shorn of its most profitable and harmful feature, the privilege of using the services of the Indians, and was reduced to some semblance of a social system.[5]

An *encomendero* held this privilege during his lifetime, passed it on to his eldest son, and then it reverted to the crown. The Spaniards, however, made every effort to turn the *encomienda* into a hereditary holding, with the hope of developing semi-feudal estates. Although later Bernal Díaz was one of the leaders of this movement, it was in the end only partly successful. The Sandoval expedition went south, touching parts of the Oaxaca Valley and then cutting through the province of Coatza-coalcos in what is now the state of Veracruz. The temples in which Bernal slept to keep away from mosquitoes probably belonged to the Zapotec empire, for he mentions skirmishes with Zapotec and Mixtec natives. In one section they found considerable gold, and this property was taken over by Sandoval. Another district was given to Luis Marín, a fellow captain and also a friend of Bernal Díaz. At this time Sandoval gave Bernal three towns named Matlatlan, Orizaba, and Ozotequipa. For some reason, Bernal did not keep them, but preferred to go on with the expedition. Later these three districts proved to be

[5] *The Encomienda in New Spain,* xiii.

profitable and he lamented: "Would to God I had accepted them."

The expedition finally reached Coatzacoalcos, where the town of Espíritu Santo was established as the headquarters for this region. The neighboring land was rich and offered excellent possibilities for development. Bernal was given three property grants, with a large number of Indians, which he was sure would make him a wealthy *hacienda* owner. He saw himself settled at last, with large holdings and plenty of Indians to develop them. About this time (1524), Cortés enacted a law requiring every married settler to bring his wife within a year and a half on penalty of forfeiting his property; those who were bachelors were forced by the same penalty to marry within that period. Bernal, who from the first was not inclined to practice celibacy, complied with the requirements of the new law.[6]

But Bernal Díaz was not fated for the life of a peaceful farmer. Hardly had he settled on his land when the constant demands of the Spaniards for tributes or taxes from the Indians caused various uprisings. One of these occurred where Bernal had his *encomienda,* and accordingly, he and three neighbors set out for the district of Cimatlan in the hope of quieting the people.

When Bernal and the three other *encomenderos* from Espíritu Santo reached the principal city of Cimatlan, they dispatched native messengers to carry word of their peaceful intentions.[7]

[6] "He [Díaz] was also no doubt living with an Indian woman at the time [1524]. There is much evidence that under similar circumstances many conquistadores married the women with whom they were living, especially if they had children." Wagner, *loc. cit.,* 195–96.

[7] Most of the Indian towns which Díaz mentions no longer exist, or they appear under different names. This is true of Espíritu Santo, although the town of Chamula, in Chiapas, where he held an *encomienda,* is still known by that name.

Before the messengers returned, however, the Spaniards were attacked by a large body of Indians armed with lances and bows and arrows. Two of Bernal's companions were killed and the third fled toward the river, where they had canoes in readiness.

Bernal, wounded and alone, managed to conceal himself behind some brush, and there, he says, he again addressed himself to heaven and implored "the aid of the Holy Virgin and beseeched Her not to let me die in the hands of these Indian dogs."[8] Then, as his fright left him and he regained his strength, Bernal rushed out. With his sword he managed to slash his way through the Indians to the river, where his surviving companion was waiting for him. Bernal and his friend were forced to hide in the woods for more than eight days, and since their neighbors in Espíritu Santo thought they were dead, their property was divided among the Spaniards according to custom. Bernal says that when they eventually turned up, their friends were happy to see them alive, but there was only disappointment on the faces of those who had received their property.

Shortly afterward, Bernal followed Captain Luis Marín in another expedition, this time into Chiapas, in southern Mexico, where they went to subjugate the Indians and to establish a Spanish colony. Bernal must have traded the little gold and jewelry he had obtained in Mexico for a horse because on this expedition he went mounted. At last he was no longer a foot soldier.

The natives of Chiapas were not vanquished as easily as Marín and Díaz expected. These Indians were part of the great Mayan race, and they assaulted the Spaniards, snaring some of the horses with lassos and trapping others with hunting nets. A number of the Spaniards were killed, and nearly all of them

[8] BDC, *cap.* clxvi.

were wounded. "Had we not been the men we were," Bernal repeated in a frequent refrain, "we might have been defeated." As usual, however, the Spaniards' superior tactics and armaments subdued the Indians.

The expedition next proceeded from the lowlands of tropical Chiapas and across the mountains toward the spot where the city of San Cristóbal de las Casas is now located. Thence they set out for Chamula, where even to this day the natives are known for their hostility. Here Bernal Díaz was to be rewarded by being given the town of Chamula in *encomienda*. Recalling this event, he wrote:

> Captain Luis Marín assigned that town [Chamula] to me, because from Mexico, Cortés had instructed that I be given something good after the area had been conquered, and also because Luis Marín was my friend . . . and even to this day I have among my posessions the *cédula de encomienda* given me and for eight years I received tributes from it.[9]

In the ranks of the expedition, difficulties suddenly arose between Marín and Diego de Godoy, a royal notary. Godoy protested against the leniency granted to a group of Indians who had revolted and had then been subdued. He demanded that the natives be punished and also forced to pay for the horses which had been lost. "I was of a different opinion," says Bernal, "and thought that since the Indians came peaceably they should not be made to suffer; and giving my opinion freely, Godoy became enraged and broke out into angry words which I considered insulting."[10] Bernal drew his sword and the two men began to duel, slashing dangerously at one another, and friends separated

[9] *Ibid.*
[10] *Ibid.*

them just in time. Angry and still shouting threats at the top of his voice, Bernal was taken to his quarters to cool off.

With his *encomienda* in Chamula definitely assigned to him, Bernal returned to Espíritu Santo with the other settlers who had been in the expedition. Here in Coatzacoalcos he began to develop his land, to plant grain, wheat, and sugar cane, all of which had been imported from Cuba.

Bernal Díaz had had enough of fighting. He now looked forward to some pleasant, peaceful years in which he could develop his land. But he had been back in Espíritu Santo only a short time when word came that Captain Cristóbal de Olid, who had been sent to Honduras, had revolted against Cortés. The news was difficult to believe, for Olid had been a faithful officer and had served well in the siege on Mexico City, but if it were true, everyone knew that Cortés would not let him go unpunished.

Cortés, they soon learned, had left Mexico City and was already approaching Coatzacoalcos on his way south to Honduras. There was hardly time to polish their swords and start out on the road to meet him. When they saw him coming, at the head of his cavalry, Cortés was smiling and in an excellent mood. He dismounted and embraced each of his veterans with his usual warmth. As they talked, he told them what Bernal had been afraid to hear. He wanted volunteers and he needed his former friends and fighting companions in the expedition. "Some of us did not want to go," Bernal said, "but there was not one of us who could say 'no' when he gave a command."[11]

Bernal hated to leave his land, yet the thought of accompanying the great Cortés into battle again was in itself a challenge to his adventurous spirit. Besides, he figured, the expedition would take only a few short months and then he would be back with

[11] *Ibid., cap.* clxxv.

new treasures and rewards. There was gold and plenty of it, he had heard, in Honduras. They might become rich men after all.

By now these hardened conquerors should have had some realistic conception of what their stakes in the New World would be, but few did. Bernal Díaz, along with the rest of them, passed from one disillusionment to another, still hopeful for their future. To these men the expedition to Honduras sounded like a very simple undertaking: a lark, when compared to the conquest of Mexico. Wasn't Cortés bringing along his musicians and tumblers and jugglers to keep him from being bored? Seldom were men more trusting and more deceived.

5 ♪ EMPTY STOMACHS, TUMBLERS AND MUSICIANS

For Bernal Díaz the expedition to Honduras had one redeeming feature which made all his subsequent hardships and privations easier to bear. Cortés commissioned him an officer for a few weeks in November, 1524, and sent him at the head of a small group of Spaniards and Indian allies to quell an uprising. He instructed Bernal to seek a peaceful settlement with the natives and if that failed, to break the revolt. Bernal never forgot the assignment.[1] "I still have in my possession" he wrote, "the authority granted to me by Cortés and countersigned by his secretary." It was not an important command, but in later years Bernal felt that it gave him the right to assume the title of captain.

We do not know why Cortés selected Bernal Díaz when there were other officers available. We can merely surmise that this uprising was a minor one and that he thought Bernal had suffi-

[1] Bernal Díaz refers to the expedition as going to Hibueras and Honduras. The former was the coastal region from the Río Dulce to the Ulúa and Naco valleys. The Río Dulce is in the Puerto Barrios region on the Atlantic seaboard of Guatemala.

cient experience to handle it. Cortés does not mention it in his long and detailed account to the king, but then he seldom spoke of any matter in which he himself was not concerned. To Bernal Díaz, however, it was a great moment in his life.

Bernal writes that he set out with thirty Spaniards and three thousand Mexicans under his command.[2] Unfortunately, he did not have much of an opportunity to prove his leadership, since his arrival on horseback with the other Spaniards was enough to frighten the natives into submission. Bernal arranged for a peaceful settlement of their grievances, warned them against another uprising, and led his men back in time to join Cortés on the expedition. He was once more a common soldier, but of course this did not prevent him from volunteering advice, at least some of which was very good. For instance, when the expedition reached the Chilapa River, the order was given to construct rafts. Bernal went to Cortés and suggested that they send five native guides to a town on their side of the river to ask the cacique for canoes. Cortés agreed to Bernal's idea, and "we not only obtained six large canoes but provisions."

As always under Cortés' leadership, the expedition to Honduras was well planned. Besides the officers, there were 140 soldiers, of whom 93 were mounted. Two of Cortés' best captains, Sandoval and Marín, were with him, and among the soldiers were many veterans. The 3,000 native allies carried the supplies, the cannons, the ammunition, and the food. There were Indian women to do the cooking, some of them common-law wives of the soldiers. In addition and as a protective measure against a possible uprising in his absence, Cortés brought with

---

[2] BDC, *cap.* clxxv. Díaz writes that he commanded three thousand Mexicans. He boasts because the entire expedition did not exceed three thousand men.

him Cuauhtémoc, the deposed leader of the Aztec capital, and the former rulers of Texcoco and Tlacopán.

Besides the musicians, jugglers, and tumblers, the retinue of Cortés included a major-domo, two stewards, a butler, a valet, a confectioner, a surgeon, a physician, a dancer, two falconers, many pages, and to be sure to have the best of food along the way, Cortés put one of his stewards in charge of a drove of pigs. A large service of gold and silver plate was also taken.

In Cortés' judgment, there was no reason why the expedition should not quickly and easily cross the southern end of Mexico, move through northern Guatemala, and reach Honduras in good order. From Indian reports and native maps, this route was the shortest and the best. It looks so even today on modern maps.

In their march on Mexico City they had passed through comparatively open country on roads that were well traveled. The ground was solid and relatively easy on the horses, even when they hit narrow, ascending trails. Despite many difficulties, there had been no unsolvable problems in moving a large body of men and equipment. But from the moment the expedition to Honduras reached Tabasco and cut across into the Petén region of Guatemala, the terrain changed radically. There were not only rivers to cross, there were also swamps in which the horses sank to their bellies; there was no open country but jungles instead; the roads were hidden trails, many of them covered by jungle growth. There were no corn milpas, and there was very little food of any kind. The weather was miserably hot and humid. It rained constantly. Ticks and thousands of mosquitoes swelled arms and legs. It seemed to the Spaniards that nothing human could live in such terrible country.

Yet in the very center of this jungle vastness was developed the great Mayan civilization, which extended its culture from

Petén to Honduras, Yucatán, Chiapas, and Tabasco. The great ruins of Tikal, the largest city in the old Mayan empire, with temples more than 220 feet high, and the ruins of Copán, in Honduras, closer to their route than Tikal, were entirely missed by the Spaniards. The Indians who provided Cortés with maps for their journey did not mention these ruins, though they doubtless knew of their existence and at the time still used some of the temples for their worship.

Sylvanus Griswold Morley, who knew this country thoroughly, called the expedition to Honduras "one of the greatest sustained efforts in military history" and added that "because of the all-but-impossible character of the intervening terrain—swamps, marshes, lagoons, many deep rivers, especially in Tabasco, trackless forests and precipitous mountain ranges—across the very heart of the Maya Old Empire, in the hot, humid Atlantic coast-plain of Middle America, the attendant hardships and privations were almost beyond mortal endurance and the army was always just one step ahead of actual starvation."[3]

Trails in this country disappear quickly as the jungle growth buries them, and natives must cut new paths with their machetes. But in the time of the Conquest it was Bernal Díaz and the soldiers who were forced, he relates, to cut their way with their swords. Often the paths they opened led to nowhere and they had to retrace their steps. Not once but many times they found themselves completely lost in the bush. To add to their difficulties, many of their guides abandoned them and they had to depend on the native maps and the compass which Pedro López, the doctor on the expedition, used to establish direction.

Bernal often went ahead with López, and once when Cortés had almost given up hope of finding a way out, it was these two

[3] *The Ancient Maya,* 117.

53

and some other soldiers who finally came upon an inhabited village. "We went at once to tell Cortés that he could be happier now, for there would be food for all," Díaz wrote.

As they pushed on and food again became scarce, a number of Spaniards and many of the native allies died. The hunger of the Indians was so great that they killed some of their companions, "barbecued them in hot coals under the ground and ate them."[4]

Among the disgruntled Spainards there was often mutinous talk, and Cortés, as usual, was blamed for leading them into this ill-fated and hazardous trip. The jugglers and the tumblers had stopped, but the musicians, ludicrously out of place, went on playing, to the anger of the soldiers. "All of us," wrote Bernal, "wanted maize to eat and not to listen to music."

As they entered the Petén region, the last of their provisions were gone. The jungle, so rich in vegetation, contained very little edible food. Bernal writes of eating wild berries and nuts, and the natives climbed sapote trees and brought down the fruit. The leaves of the *ramón,* or breadnut tree, provided fodder for the horses and the nuts were ground into a black flour for making bread, but there was not enough of these things for a hungry army. The men shot wild turkeys, pheasants, and other fowl, but again, the number which foraging parties were able to get was limited.

Bernal stayed close to Pedro López, the doctor, and watched him as he read the compass and tried to follow the directions indicated on the roughly drawn native maps. The heat grew even more humid and intense, and now the jungle became like a darkened chamber, for the giant mahogany and sapote trees shut out the sun almost completely. Not a step could be taken without making a clearance, and the entangling vines of the lianas were always across the path.

[4] BDC, *cap.* clxxv.

As Bernal Díaz suffered along with the others, he must often have wondered why he had been foolish enough to come on this expedition. He had been happy on his land and he regretted he had ever left. It would be ironic, he thought, after the conquest of Mexico, to perish from starvation and disease in this darkened jungle prison.

The smile of the ever confident Cortés disappeared; even Sandoval and Marín, tough hardened veterans, were almost hopelessly defeated by the jungle. The cannons, the guns, and all their military equipment, including the excellent strategy of Cortés, were useless here in the wilds. They needed food desperately and it had to be found soon or they would perish. By the map—if they were going in the right direction and if the compass was accurate—there was a town not very far ahead. Cortés summoned Bernal Díaz, the opportunist, the man who always looked out for himself, who seemed to have an uncanny facility for finding food. He instructed Bernal to locate this settlement and to bring back all the food available. Cortés' judgment in selecting Díaz for this mission was as good as usual. Bernal and the group that accompanied him, after four days of traveling, finally reached a sizable town and lost no time in extracting from the caciques promises of food.

While they were there, two other Spaniards arrived with a letter from Cortés, advising Bernal that he had broken camp and was moving forward. Cortés informed Bernal that if he found food he was to meet them on their way as quickly as possible, for the condition of the soldiers was now even more grim. With the help of the caciques, the party gathered all the corn, beans, and honey they could lay hands on. Then, after they had had their fill of food, they set out to join Cortés.

In the meantime, Cortés had ordered the construction of a bridge over a river they were forced to cross. On the night this bridge was finished, Bernal Díaz arrived with 130 loads of corn (an Indian load was roughly 50 pounds), 80 fowl, beans, honey, salt, eggs, and fruit. Since it was dark and his return was antici- pated, the soldiers surrounded him like crazed men and seized all of the food for themselves before they could be stopped, leaving nothing for Cortés and the officers.

The annoyed Cortés summoned Bernal and reprimanded him for not guarding the provisions so that they could be rationed evenly. "I then told him that even if he himself had been there, he could not have stopped the soldiers, for hunger knew no law," Bernal wrote.

Cortés, who was with Sandoval, soon lost his ill humor, Bernal reported: "Cortés spoke to me with much kindness and said: 'My esteemed friend and brother, did you not by any chance leave something hidden in the road for yourself, that you can share with me and Sandoval? If so, for the love of me, tell us.' I was moved by Cortés' words and by his pleading look. Then Sando- val said to me: 'I swear to you that I also haven't a handful of corn left.' "

Bernal Díaz could not refuse them. He had to admit that he had taken necessary measures to provide for himself and that there was enough for all three of them. "I then told them," he wrote, "that we had best wait until everyone was asleep and I would bring out what I had concealed."

Bernal revealed to them that he had hidden "twelve loads of corn, twenty fowl, three jars of honey, beans, salt and some fruit, which should be sufficient for us three as well as my servants." The three embraced each other at the good news, and after mid- night, Sandoval accompanied Bernal and his servants to the place where the provisions were cached. Bernal was impressed that Sandoval himself should go instead of sending his soldiers, "but he did not want to trust them," he explained, "such was the hunger of the men."

In addition to the provisions he had hidden, Bernal had also brought from the town two Indian women, "and I gave one of them to Sandoval," he said of his increasing generosity.[5]

The following day, continuing their march, they struck deep swamps again. The horses sank to above the saddles and only by pulling them were the men able to get them through. When they were once more on firmer ground, Cortés called for Bernal and instructed him to take an advance party to the settlement for additional food. Bernal reached the village that night and in the morning sent three of the soldiers and a hundred natives loaded with corn and other provisions. This time the party was met far in front by Cortés, Sandoval, and Marín, who saw to it that the food was distributed evenly among all the men and officers.

On reaching the settlement Cortés talked with the *principales,* and after some questioning, they informed him that other bearded foreigners had established quarters at a distance of eight days' journey and that they had three ships in the harbor. This news encouraged Cortés, and he now obtained new native maps to follow the route which would take them there.

He next sent an advance expedition to open the route and to collect additional provisions from towns which were reported to be located along the river. Probably for diplomatic reasons, he placed Diego de Mazariegos, a nephew of the king's treasurer, at the head of the advance group. Before Mazariegos departed, Cortés told him in confidence that since he was new to the country and inexperienced in dealing with the Indians, he would be accompanied by Bernal Díaz.

[5] *Ibid., cap.* clxxvi.

According to Bernal, he did go with Mazariegos, and the latter listened to his advice. Bernal says that he mentions this, not to boast, but to put it on record. Whether or not Mazariegos heeded Bernal's advice, at least this part of the expedition was successful. They returned with large quantities of provisions, as well as tribal *principales,* who came to wait upon Cortés.

The entire army eventually reached the large settlement of Acalan, and while they rested before proceeding farther south, Cortés heard of a conspiracy between Cuauhtémoc, the other two deposed rulers, and the Indians. That there was some truth to this intrigue is quite probable, for it was not in Cortés' character to act harshly without justifiable motives. It does not seem likely, however, that the threat of an uprising was serious, but Cortés and his men had had enough difficulties and hardships to make the possibility of trouble with the natives an added burden. Bernal describes the situation:

> Their confession was that perceiving that we marched without precaution, that discontent prevailed, that many of our soldiers were sick, and that provisions were so scarce and considering also the uncertainty of our fate and destination, they had decided that dying at once was preferable to going with us any farther. They had therefore resolved to try their fortunes, and fall upon us at the passage of some river or marsh. . . . Cuauhtémoc denied, however, that the whole of the Mexican force was concerned in this plot, or that it would have ever been, to his knowledge, carried out.

Bernal, who had a liking for Cuauhtémoc and had admired his valiant defense of the Aztec capital, was not in accordance with the sentence pronounced by Cortés. There was not, he felt, sufficient proof to warrant execution, yet neither he nor any of the soldiers or officers protested at the time. As he stood watching

58

while the noose was being put around Cuauhtémoc's neck, he heard the emperor cry out: "Oh, Malinche, I know now what it was to trust to thy false promises! Why dost thou kill me so unjustly? Better had I taken my own life when thou entered the city. God will demand of thee the reasons!"[6]

The signal was given, the rope pulled, and from a high branch of a ceiba tree swayed the body of the last emperor of the Aztecs. A few minutes later the ruler of Tacuba and several others were killed the same way. "Their deaths were not justified," Bernal said, "and all of us soldiers were in accord in this sentiment. . . . It gave me great sorrow to see them die in this manner, for they had been kind and good to me and on one occasion on the road, they had provided me with Indians, who brought fodder for my horse."[7]

The torturing of Cuauhtémoc and his execution on insufficient evidence have never been forgotten. In all of Mexico there is not a statue or monument of Cortés, but one of the largest and most imposing ones on the Avenida de la Reforma in Mexico City was erected in honor of Cuauhtémoc.

As the expedition continued farther south they approached a more populated area where food again became plentiful. There were fowl, maize, and beans, and now for the first time Bernal Díaz tasted a *tamal,* which, he said, was "something new to us, and we liked the taste of it, and all the other food we found."[8] While they pushed on, they shortly struck open country and large plains without trees. Here were wild deer, of which the horsemen hunted down and killed more than twenty. Next they

[6] *Ibid., cap.* clxxvii.

[7] *Ibid.*

[8] This matter of tasting *tamales* for the first time is strange, since they were common in Mexico long before the Conquest.

met natives carrying a recently slaughtered mountain lion and some iguanas, which, according to Bernal, "were very good to eat."

The expedition had started in October of 1524 and they had been on the trail more than six months and were now in the midst of the rainy season. But presently, with better native guides to direct them, they came upon a large body of water with an island in the distance. This was the lake of Petén and its island of Flores, inhabited by Mayas. "Its houses and lofty temples," said Bernal, "glistened in the sun and they could be seen two leagues away."

The Mayas of this area received them well and provided them with food, but Bernal, at least for the time being, lost his appetite. He fell ill of fever and sunstroke and would have liked to stop and rest in these friendly surroundings. Cortés was anxious to push on, however, for they were not far from the Río Dulce and the town of Nito, where Spaniards were reported to have a settlement.[9]

Sick as he was, Bernal lagged behind, sometimes carried by his servants but walking most of the time. His great stamina did not fail him, and soon he was well enough to feel the pangs of hunger, for again the army was out of provisions. "Never in my life did I feel so depressed in my heart," he wrote, "when I found there was no food for myself or my people, and I sick with fever. And all this on the eve of Our Lord's resurrection. Our plight was pitiful for we would have been content to have a little maize to eat on Easter day."[10]

[9] In 1949, Edwin Shook of the University of Pennsylvania and I located, on the Río Dulce, what we believe was once the town of Nito. Bernal Díaz' description of the place is precise. The area does not appear to have changed greatly during the past four hundred years.

[10] BDC, *cap.* clxxviii.

Cortés called together his veterans and beseeched them to search for food. He appointed Bernal Díaz to lead one of the foraging parties and sent them out in various directions. Bernal, with five soldiers and two guides, crossed rivers and swamps and came upon a settlement where there was plenty of maize stored, as well as fowl and squash. "We captured four Indians and three women and despite everything, we had an excellent Easter," he remembered.

After a march of many days they reached a hill from which they had a view of the mouth of the Río Dulce. They crossed to the other side and came upon what was then the town of Nito and there saw unmistakable signs of the presence of Spaniards. Sandoval was ordered to sail up the river in native boats and explore ahead. The river was wide and deep, with an air of mystery about its emerald-green water. On both sides the banks were a mass of jungle growth, with tall ceiba and mahogany trees in the background. Wild orchids were growing on the branches of the mangroves and kapoks. Farther along there were cliffs of bedded limestone, and occasionally an alligator lurked in the shadows.

The river now widened into a gulf and merged with Lake Izabal. Later, when Cortés sailed up the gulf, he was almost certain he had struck a body of water which connected the Pacific and Atlantic oceans. But at the present moment Sandoval was more interested in locating the Spaniards of Nito. He finally found a small group of them searching for food in a clearing along the banks. They were startled to learn that the great Cortés was in the expedition, and they advised Sandoval of the fate of Cristóbal de Olid. He had been killed, they said, some months previously by Francisco de las Casas, one of Cortés' own men, in another of those Spanish intrigues that permeated the Conquest.

The expedition to Honduras had been undertaken to punish Olid, to stop the revolt of the settlers, and to re-establish the authority of Cortés. For this purpose Bernal Díaz and his companions had come hundreds of miles, had brought cannons, arms, and ammunition, but instead of a Spanish colony in rebellion, they found the Spaniards suffering from famine, beaten, and defeated.

Bernal Díaz now hoped they would soon return to Mexico he to his land and Cortés to the capital. But more than two years were to pass from the day Bernal left Coatzacoalcos to the time he again set foot on his property.

6   *MORE COMPLAINTS AND BIGGER BANQUETS*

Somewhere in Honduras, Bernal Díaz celebrated his twenty-ninth birthday. The fire of youth was gone. He felt old and tired, and he was sick from fever and dysentery. Eventually, he regained his strength and joined the forces of Pedro de Alvarado in helping to quell a native rebellion in the Guatemalan highlands.

Presently they reached the valley where the city of Antigua is now located.[1] As they passed Volcano Fuego in the summer of 1526, they experienced a series of earthquakes, some so violent, says Bernal, that a number of soldiers were thrown to the ground.

This valley was to be Bernal's future home; here he was to live, raise his large family, and write the history of the Conquest.

---

[1] The first capital of Guatemala was established by Alvarado at Iximché, which was also the chief town of the Cakchiquel Indians. Iximché was called Patinamit by the Spaniards. After they were forced out of Patinamit, the Spaniards moved to near-by Tecpán, and not until several years later did they move to the valley of Almolonga, near present-day Antigua. See Hubert Howe Bancroft, *History of Central America,* II, 654.

Yet at the moment his thoughts were far from settling in this country; he was as anxious as the others to get to Mexico. But he did take back a souvenir from Guatemala—an arrow wound he suffered in a battle with the natives.

When he finally returned to Mexico City, Bernal stayed at the house of Andrés de Tapia, where his friend Sandoval sent him new clothes, as well as cacao beans, which were still being used as currency.[2]

Soon after, Bernal Díaz and several *encomenderos,* accompanied by Sandoval and Tapia, appeared before the new governor, Marcos de Aguilar. Sandoval introduced them to the governor and described the services the men had rendered to the king. At this verbal hearing the *encomenderos* sought to reestablish their rights to their lands and to request additional Indians from the valley of Mexico. Aguilar, a sickly old man (Bernal could not resist commenting on the fact that the governor was being breast fed), listened to their petition, promised to do what he could, but maintained he had no judicial right to assign them Indians.[3]

It did not take Bernal Díaz long to realize that he was not going to get any satisfaction from the governor. Instead of the additional rewards he had anticipated, he soon found he was being forced out of his *encomiendas* in Tlapa and Chamula, and the other land he had possessed was also in jeopardy and might be lost. He concluded that if he was going to fight for his rights, he would have to stay in the capital, where with the help of Cortés and Sandoval he might receive other *encomiendas.*

As the months passed, Bernal perceived that neither Cortés nor Sandoval could help him get the spoils he felt he deserved.

[2] BDC, *cap.* cxciii.
[3] *Ibid.*

In disgust he watched while new arrivals from Spain came with *cédulas* of land grants which should have been turned over to the veteran conquerors.

For a time the death of Aguilar, the governor, gave the men some hope that the king and the Council of the Indies might relent and return Cortés to power, but they were in for another disappointment. Alonso de Estrada, the king's treasurer and an enemy of Cortés, was named governor, with full authority to rule over New Spain. Bernal Díaz and those loyal to Cortés were indignant. To add to their anger, Cortés was completely ignored by the new governor and some of his friends insulted. Bernal and many of the conquerors, including some who had previously criticized Cortés, now came to his defense. Díaz says there were even some hardheaded ruffians who were willing to organize an open revolt and, if necessary, to break away from Spain and establish an independent nation. Díaz furthermore states that Cortés called these men traitors and had them arrested.[4]

Yet had Cortés given the word, it is quite possible that such a course could have been followed. Veterans like Bernal Díaz, who had fought and suffered great hardships, were becoming more and more embittered by the encroachment of their rights and by the minor role to which they were relegated in the affairs of New Spain. They besought Cortés to act. But Cortés refused and retired from the great city he had conquered to his home in Coyoacán. About this time, the king dispatched a commission called the *Real Audiencia de Nueva España* to investigate fully Estrada's reign, as well as certain charges made against Cortés. The commission was empowered with orders to return Cortés to Spain, willingly or in irons. But this step was hardly necessary, for even before the *Audiencia* arrived Cortés had decided

----

[4] *Ibid., cap.* cxciv.

to leave for Spain with Sandoval and present his case to the king.

Shortly before Cortés left, Bernal had been busy on his own account and had received from Governor Estrada on April 3, 1528, in *encomienda,* three towns: Gualpitan and Micapa in the province of Cimatlan and the town of Popoloatan in the province of Cintla. But Bernal was either not satisfied with these grants or felt he deserved more, for when the first *Real Audiencia* established itself in Mexico City, he was among those who requested additional land. His petition, however, was denied.

In Spain, Cortés had successfully defended himself and was raised to the rank of a nobleman and had been named governor general of New Spain. Upon his return to Mexico, however, he found that his titles were more impressive than the authority they carried. Cortés was considered by the king and his advisers to be entirely too powerful ever to rule alone. He was permitted to make recommendations, but not to administer the laws. For this purpose, the *Real Audiencia,* composed of a *presidente* and *oidores,* had been appointed.

During the next six or eight years we hear little of Bernal Díaz. But on one occasion when he appeared before the second *Audiencia,* he was named *visitador* to the provinces of Coatzacoalcos and Tabasco. He also served terms as *procurador síndico* of Espíritu Santo and, later, as *regidor.*

It can be assumed from the fact that he held these positions that he spent considerable time in Coatzacoalcos and Tabasco and in the provinces of Cimatlan and Cintla, where he had land. He was frequently in Mexico City, too, appearing before the *Audiencia* on behalf of the districts he represented but mostly on behalf of himself. For Bernal Díaz was ever hopeful, always sure that a new turn of events would eventually bring him richer rewards.

This illusion of better things to come dominated all the conquerors and especially Bernal. What ailed the conquerors of Mexico? Why did Bernal Díaz and so many of his companions protest for so long that they had not been justly reimbursed for the part they had played in the Conquest?

None of them were badly off, but few, if any, of the original groups felt they had been amply rewarded. Some of them lost the land which had been given them, but what irked them was to see that the newly arrived settlers from Spain were given greater consideration and favors.

The Spanish court attempted to enforce laws abolishing enslavement of the natives and made a sincere effort to stop corruption, but bureaucracy, political intrigue, and lack of proper communications prevented many of the idealistic reforms which had been planned. Some of the new laws Spain wanted carried out were not applicable to a frontier country; others were beyond enforcement.

Throughout the sixteenth century, when the president and members of the *Audiencia* received a law not to their liking, they usually placed the royal decree above their heads and said, *"Obedezco pero no cumplo."* I obey but do not comply.

The laws which disturbed Bernal Díaz and many of his companions were those which gave freedom to prisoners of war who had been enslaved and to Indians held in *encomienda*. If these were laws which for the moment could not be enforced, they could not be ignored, either, primarily because of the presence of Bartolomé de las Casas, a Dominican priest.

Las Casas, as an eighteen-year-old law student at the University of Salamanca, had had his own slave and later owned many more on land he possessed in the New World. Eventually, however, he released them, turned to the priesthood, and became not only the great defender of the natives but also a villain in the eyes of the conquerors. Bernal Díaz learned to fear and to hate him, and the two clashed frequently, once before the Spanish court.

Las Casas had no sympathy for the ambitions of such men as Bernal Díaz. He had only one objective: to free the native slaves and break up the system of *encomiendas*. To accomplish this mission, Las Casas began work about 1537 on a damaging and, as far as the conquerors were concerned, vicious report which he called *Brevísima relación de la destrucción de las Indias* (*A Brief History of the Destruction of the Indies*). In attempting to attain freedom for the Indians, however, Las Casas contributed to a grave error: the introduction of Negro slaves into Mexico, Central America, and other parts of the New World. Las Casas lived long enough to admit his mistake, but by then it was too late.

The system of *encomiendas* was a natural outgrowth of conquest. There was not enough gold for everyone, and Cortés early recognized the importance of developing the land. With this in mind he had urged the king not to allow a ship to leave Spain without seeds and plants. He made it mandatory for every *encomendero* to plant agricultural products of every type. Soon sugar cane, oranges, and peaches, as well as other fruits and vegetables heretofore unknown in the New World, began to flourish in the gardens and land of the *encomenderos*.

What were the responsibilities of an *encomendero*? Lesley Byrd Simpson, an able historian who has delved deeply into the *encomienda* system, says:

> The royal *cédulas,* which created the *encomienda,* attempted to make of the conquistador a guardian of the Indians and a sort of lay missionary—responsibility which he was little fitted to assume—

68

and it should come as no surprise to learn that he took his spiritual obligation lightly. And yet I find it difficult to completely swallow the image of the scowling monster, whip in hand, so fiercely denounced by interested ecclesiastics and so ably painted by Diego Rivera.[5]

There were good and bad *encomenderos,* some who treated the Indians with consideration and kindness, others who abused them, overworked them, and were cruel. Yet at its best the *encomienda* was based on a feudal ideal. The *encomendero* was the master and the ruler of his estate; the Indians, his servants and workers, were subject to his will.

But if the conquerors who supported this system were responsible for many abuses, Las Casas also realized that the Catholic church and the order of which he was a member, and with which he often differed, shared some of the guilt. Yet the majority of the priests were kind and befriended the natives. The Indians accepted and took quickly to the new religion the Spaniards introduced, and the priests had no trouble in getting all the native labor they needed to construct their churches, convents, and monasteries.

What kind of an *encomendero* was Bernal Díaz? Although he probably lost his temper occasionally, he was not cruel. He was kindly disposed toward the natives and in one specific instance, for which we have documentation, he came to their defense in a long legal battle. He was sick and old at the time, yet he fought with the same ardor and persistence he possessed on the battlefield. Writing about this litigation, Professor Simpson points out that this suit

[5] "Bernal Díaz del Castillo, Encomendero," *Hispanic American Historical Review,* Vol. XVII (1937), 101.

shows clearly the identity of interest of Bernal Díaz and the Indians of his *encomienda,* for any diminution of their revenue-producing lands meant a corresponding loss to him; it also shows that the Indians regarded him as their natural protector and that he regarded himself in the same light. It shows, moreover, that the *audiencia* concurred in his opinion and, by reversing its original stand, regarded his argument as generally valid. I might add, by way of postscript, that had it not been for the stout fight put up by Bernal Díaz the Indians would assuredly have lost their lands.[6]

And the Mexican historian Genaro García reports that Díaz

treated in an excellent manner the Indians of the towns he had in *encomienda,* and for this they praised him in all parts, and the Dominican priests, always so severe and demanding, held him up as a model for other *encomenderos;* it can be affirmed that there were no other towns where the Indians received better treatment and were forced to pay less tributes than those of Bernal Díaz.[7]

Yet there can be no question that Bernal enjoyed the fruits of the feudal system and fought hard for its continuation. From the first, neither Bernal Díaz nor any of his companions ever considered the Indians anything but slaves.[8] He had the typical conqueror's intolerance of them. He was seldom sentimental about them, and he seems always to have been firm in dealing with them. However, one of the interesting facts of the post-Conquest period is not that the Spaniards treated the Indians

[6] *Ibid.,* 106.

[7] *Bernal Díaz del Castillo: noticias bio-bibliográficas,* 34.

[8] See a petition from Bernal Díaz to the Council of the Indies protesting the liberation of Indian slaves, dated February 1, 1549, in Lesley Byrd Simpson, *Studies in the Administration of the Indians in New Spain,* IV, 32.

badly or cruelly, but that in many cases they acted kindly toward them. At least the Indians were able to retain part of their culture and were not wiped out.

Fray Bartolomé de las Casas predicted that this would happen to the Indians of New Spain and the Spanish colonies. "From the year 1518," he wrote, "until today which is now in the year 1542, has swelled up and come to a head all the wickedness, injustice, violence and tyranny which the Christians have done in the Indies. . . . I affirm it is as very certain and approved that during these forty years owing to the aforesaid tyrannies and infernal works of the Christians more than twelve million souls, men, women and children, have perished unjustly and tyrannically; and in truth I believe I should not be overstepping the mark in saying fifteen million . . . ."[9]

Las Casas was a fanatic reformer and was devoted to the cause for which he was fighting. Yet he must also have realized that unless he painted an extremely dark picture of conditions in the colonies, the king and the Council of the Indies would not be sufficiently impressed to issue the reform laws he advocated. Las Casas was furthermore convinced that if the abuses of the Spaniards continued, the entire Indian population would perish.

Many of Las Casas' predictions did not come true. Today the Indian population in Mexico and in most of Central America, particularly in Guatemala, is greater than it was in his time. In many villages the Indians have retained their culture and their customs, much as these were four hundred years ago. And

---

[9] *Brevísima relación de la destrucción de las Indias,* 69–70. On Las Casas, see Lewis Hanke's *The Spanish Struggle for Justice in the Conquest of America.* For a realistic analysis of Indian mortality, see Borah, *op. cit.,* and Sherburne F. Cook and Woodrow Wilson Borah, *The Indian Population of Central Mexico, 1531–1610.*

nowhere in Latin America was it necessary to establish Indian reservations.

Unquestionably, there was a great deal of truth to what Las Casas observed and reported upon. He was one of the men most responsible for the betterment of the natives in the post-Conquest period. But this did not endear him to Bernal Díaz and the other Spanish settlers. Between 1526, when Bernal returned to Mexico from Honduras, and 1535, the issue of slavery and the Indian *encomiendas* grew in intensity.

It became no longer a question of whether the Spaniards could increase the number of their native servants, but whether they could hold on to those they already had. Bernal Díaz was clearly embittered at what was taking place, and he was sure his problems and those of his companions would never have become so serious if Cortés had remained in power. With the unsympathetic *Audiencia* now in control, it was a different story, and Bernal Díaz cannot be blamed for the attitude he assumed.

His position was this: he had fought as a soldier of the king, yet the crown had not paid him a salary, had not provided him with guns, ammunition, or clothes; he had found it necessary to buy everything—food, wine, even medicine—for himself; he had seldom complained of the hardships and danger he had endured since he landed in the New World; he had seen friends die at his side and he had witnessed the barbaric death of others on sacrificial altars. "Of the soldiers who came with Cortés from Cuba only five of us remain," he writes. "The rest died in battle or were sacrificed to the native idols. And when people ask me where they are buried, I say, they are in the stomachs of the Indians who ate them or they were fed to the tigers and other wild animals they had in cages. I furthermore say that their names should be written in letters of gold, for they died such cruel deaths in order to serve God and His Majesty and to give

72

light to those who are in darkness." Then he adds, more realistically, "and also to acquire that wealth which most of us came to search for."[10]

The possibility of gaining such wealth had been snatched away from him. He was also at this time having trouble retaining his land and the Indians he held in *encomienda,* and what was even more difficult for him to accept was that the prisoners he felt he had rightfully seized in battle and made his slaves might be subject to future loss. Yet when the slave problem became an important issue, Bernal took a stand against the enslavement of additional natives because of the many abuses being committed and because "among us men, not all of us are good."

He recounts that while he was a *regidor* in Coatzacoalcos, the branding iron used on the slaves was in his possession, that he and one of his companions secretly destroyed it, and that they were among the first to do such a thing. "We then wrote to the president of the *Audiencia,* and told him how we had broken the branding iron, and urged him to prohibit the future use of it, so there would be no more slaves in New Spain."[11]

This statement may be considered as salve to his conscience, for Bernal was not consistent in his feelings toward slavery. On some occasions he was opposed to it; at other times, specifically when there was any possible danger of losing his own slaves, he felt that slavery was essential.

What appeared to irk him more than the slavery issue was the realization that others, whom he thought far less deserving of royal acknowledgment than he, were receiving more valuable *encomiendas:* "They [the *Audiencia*] gave rights and privileges to their relatives, and others who did not deserve to have them."

[10] BDC, *cap.* ccx.
[11] *Ibid., cap.* ccxiii.

It is doubtful, however, that Bernal and his companions were as poor as they said they were. Complaints and protests from the conquerors were the rule, not the exception. Even Cortés pleaded poverty.

The Mexican historian Joaquín Ramírez Cabañas states that when Viceroy Antonio de Mendoza ordered an inquiry into the economic conditions of the conquerors and settlers, "of two thousand three hundred and eighty-five persons who were questioned, less than ten or twenty did not declare themselves to be in extreme necessity." Among those who appeared on the register were Francisco de Montejo (later the conqueror and governor of Yucatán), Francisco Vásquez de Coronado, Captain Luis Marín, and Juan Xuares, the brother-in-law of Cortés. "It is well known and notorious," adds Cabañas, "that during the middle of the sixteenth century, many of the conquerors were rich, yet they never lost an opportunity to declare themselves poor in order to get additional favors,"[12]

While Bernal Díaz did lose some of the original *encomiendas* given him by Cortés, he still retained large property grants and many Indians. At the same time, it is difficult to understand why, if everything was going so well for him, in the end he abandoned his holdings in Mexico and moved to Guatemala, as he did in later years.

The series of *fiestas* and banquets staged in Mexico City in 1538 to celebrate the Spanish king's visit to France indicates that Bernal and the other veteran conquerors were not having such a bad time of it. Bernal describes these activities in great detail and compares them to Roman feasts.

During the week of festivities there were bullfights, tournaments between knights in armor, cockfights, native dances,

[12] Cabañas, I, 17.

horse races, and sham battles between Turks and Christians. All day long there was music. There was no sign of poverty, according to Bernal's description, for the women in the windows and in the balconies overlooking the plaza "were attired in the richest clothes of silk and of damask and they all wore precious stones."

The *fiestas* helped to overcome the strained relations which had been developing between Cortés and Mendoza, the king's viceroy. Previously there had been a conflict between the two about who should have precedence at public functions. Just before the *fiestas,* the protocol finally agreed upon required that when the viceroy dined in the home of Cortés, he should sit at the head of the table and both should be served simultaneously; when Cortés went to the viceroy's house, the seats were placed, not at the head of the table, but at each side. It was also decided that when they met on the street, on foot or on horseback, Cortés would yield the right side to Mendoza, but if they went to church at the same time, they would kneel on the same cushion.

At the time of the celebration two banquets were planned, the first to be given by Cortés and the second by Mendoza. Both were attended by hundreds of guests, including Bernal Díaz, who excused his bad memory for not describing all that was served, "for there was so much of it, I cannot remember all."

For the first course there were two or three salads of different types, after which roasted goat meat and whole hams, cooked Genoese style, were served. Next came quail and doves and stuffed roosters and chickens, then *manjar blanco,* a dish consisting of the breasts of fowl mixed with sugar, milk, and rice flour. Squash and partridges, followed by pickled quail, made up the fifth course. Finally, says Bernal, they changed the tablecloths and began all over again, this time with fish, lamb, pork, venison, and native fruits of all kinds. There was wine, of course, in

75

golden goblets and flowing generously from fountains, "but there were so many drunks, they broke the fountains which fell to the floor," Bernal added, then struck it out of his manuscript.[13]

There were musicians at the head of each of the two main tables, as well as jesters and wits who said "many things of Cortés and the viceroy that made us laugh." Then Bernal, the great detailist, continues: "And I have not mentioned the olives, radishes, artichokes and cheeses which were served." Once more he censored his own manuscript and crossed out "There were some who were so drunk and said aloud such things, they had to be removed from the banquet by force."[14]

Bernal, with his inexhaustible curiosity, noticed that at the viceroy's banquet none of the gold or silver dishes disappeared, but at the one given by Cortés more than a hundred pieces were missing. "I soon discovered the reason why nothing was stolen at the viceroy's," he explains. "His major-domo saw to it that an Indian guarded each place at the table, and when dishes with uneaten food were taken by the guests to their various homes, the Indians followed and brought back the plates."[15] He reported that among the stolen articles were silver salt shakers, knives, tablecloths, and napkins.

About this time Cortés suggested to Bernal Díaz that he go with him to Spain and there place his fight for land and Indians before the king and the Council of the Indies. Bernal needed no urging, for, unable to get any satisfaction from the *Audiencia,* he had already been contemplating such a trip. The more he thought about it, the more he realized the importance of making this visit. He well knew that whatever honors and concessions

[13] BDC, *cap.* cci.
[14] *Ibid.*
[15] *Ibid.*

76

Cortés had received were due to his previous trip to Spain. This was equally true of other conquerors, including Pedro de Alvarado, who had returned from the Spanish court with the title of *adelantado* of Guatemala.

In Spain anything was possible if the king was favorably impressed. Perhaps he, too, might be amply reimbursed. It was clear that the king and queen had never failed to reward justly one of their subjects who had served them well. But first Bernal Díaz knew he had to prove his case. The best way was through a *probanza de servicios y méritos,* a petition of proof of services rendered and accomplishments. Such verification usually came through the sworn testimony of witnesses who established the contentions in the petition.

Whom could Bernal Díaz call upon to be his witnesses and to testify in his behalf? There were his friends, Captain Luis Marín, Cristóbal Hernández, Martín Vásquez, Miguel Sánchez de Gascón, and others.

As he sat thinking, he picked up pen and paper and began to write a brief outline for his *servicios y méritos.* When he read over what he had written, he was certain this *probanza* would open the doors to an audience with the king. This outline was the bare beginning of his history of the Conquest, on which rested his future fame.

7 ❧ ON BEHALF OF BERNAL DÍAZ

BERNAL DÍAZ soon found that it was easier to be a conqueror than to prove it.

During the very early days of the post-Conquest period the king had acceded to a request from Mexico and had prohibited "attorneys and men learned in the law from setting foot in the country, on grounds that experience had shown they would be sure by their evil practices to disturb the peace of the community."[1] This ban was not enforced, however, and in 1539 there were not only *licenciados* on the board of the *Audiencia,* but bureaucratic machinery, with civil servants, had been established. Everything had to pass through the proper channels and all pleas had to be written by *escribanos,* or notaries. For the historian delving into the past, these documents are valuable; for the conquerors and settlers of New Spain, they were a troublesome chore.

[1] Quoted in Prescott, *History of the Conquest of Mexico,* 637.

Bernal had at this time roughly drafted, in his almost illegible scrawl, the case he wanted to present before the king and the Council of the Indies. He had selected the questions to be asked with considerable thought, and he had lined up witnesses who had known him through the years. His objective was to substantiate that he had been a conqueror, that he had served the king and at his own expense, that certain Indians given to him in *encomienda* had been taken from him, and that he had not been justly compensated for his years of service.

He now learned he could not go ahead with his *probanza* without the approval of the *Audiencia*. He therefore sought a notary, dictated to him his petition for approval, and, bringing his credentials, appeared before Antonio de Turcios, the secretary of the *Audiencia*. The petition, still preserved, along with his *probanza,* in the archives at Seville, Spain, reads as follows:

To the Illustrious Señor Don Antonio de Mendoza,
Viceroy and Governor of New Spain:
Very Powerful Sir:
I, Bernal Díaz, one of the first discoverers and conquerors of New Spain, say that I intend to make a *probanza* of services rendered to Our Majesty during the discovery, the conquest and the bringing of peace to New Spain; in accordance I hereby entreat Our Majesty to give the order to receive my witnesses so that they may be examined and questioned in regard to my services. After the depositions of these said witnesses have been taken, I ask that the proper authority and judicial decree of the *Audiencia* be granted to the testimony of these witnesses in proof of good faith. In the name of all this, I implore and ask of your royal office that this be done so that full justice may be carried out.[2]

[2] Cabañas, III, 312. The original documents are in the AGI, Seville.

After presenting this petition, Bernal waited until the *Audiencia* granted his request and ordered him to appear, with the witnesses, before the *alcalde ordinario* of the city of Mexico.[3] The *alcalde* was Juan Jaramillo, who had been with Bernal on the expedition to Honduras, and he now set the date for the hearing. On February 10, Bernal appeared with his first witness, Cristóbal Hernández, in the office of the *alcalde*.[4]

Before the proceedings began, Bernal presented to the notary as evidence two *cédulas* for land and Indians given to him; one authorization was signed by Cortés in 1522, and the other, dated 1528, was signed by Alonso de Estrada, then governor of New Spain. The first *cédula* granted Bernal in *encomienda* the towns of Tlapa and Potuchan in the province of Cimatlan.[5] The second granted the towns of Gualpitan, Micapa, and Popoloatan, along with the Indians of each place.[6]

With these deeds recorded, the notary called on Cristóbal Hernández to testify.[7] Sitting near by, Bernal watched and listened as Hernández stood before a crucifix, made the Sign of the Cross with the fingers of his right hand, and then swore and promised to tell the truth in the name of Our Savior.[8]

After giving his name and age, he was asked the first question:

---

[3] An *alcalde ordinario* was inferior to an *alcalde mayor,* who was chief civil magistrate, or administrator.

[4] Cabañas, III, 313.

[5] *Ibid.,* 318.

[6] *Ibid.,* 319.

[7] *Ibid.*

[8] The manner in which witnesses were sworn was described to me by Don Miguel Prado, then chief justice of the Supreme Court of Guatemala, who had in his office a crucifix, dating back to 1650, which was used to swear witnesses in Guatemala.

"Do you know Bernal Díaz and for how long have you known him in these parts?"

"I have been acquainted with him for twenty years, more or less," Hernández replied.

"Do you know," he was asked next, "or have you seen or have you heard that Bernal Díaz came to New Spain from the island of Cuba and that he helped to discover the coast of this country and that he did this without receiving a salary from His Majesty or from any other source, and that when he came on this expedition he was in the company of Captain Francisco de Córdoba? Answer to what you know."

"I affirm this to be the truth," Hernández testified.

"But how do you know?"

"Because I was on this expedition with Captain Córdoba and Bernal Díaz was one of those present. For this reason I can vouch that all of the rest of the second question is as stated."

"Is it true and to your knowledge that this said Bernal Díaz, in the aforementioned voyage of discovery, suffered many hardships and great dangers and that in the town of Potonchan [Champoton], he sustained two serious wounds and was on the point of death?"

"Both he and all of us suffered great hardships on landings made along the coast," Hernández said, and then added, "though I do not remember if he was wounded at the time or not."

"Now after he returned to the island of Cuba from this expedition of discovery, did he accompany the Marqués del Valle, Don Hernán Cortés, when the latter came to conquer and pacify New Spain? And did he do so without salary or payment of any kind? Is it also true that he labored with great force and energy in the conquest of this land? Speak what you know on these matters."

"I affirm all which is asked in these questions to be the truth because I was present during all this period," he replied.

"To your knowledge did Bernal Díaz come with the Marqués del Valle to Mexico City and take part in its conquest and was the said Bernal Díaz under the command of Pedro de Alvarado at the time of the conquest of said city? Furthermore, did Bernal Díaz suffer great hardships, hunger and sustain many wounds up to the day the Aztec emperor was seized and afterwards?"

"Yes, I know it to be so."

"How do you know, Cristóbal Hernández?"

"Because I was present. He, Bernal Díaz, served His Majesty well throughout the period of the Conquest and he did everything which can be expected from a man, and not only do I say this, but it is common knowledge."

"Following the conquest of Mexico City, did Bernal Díaz go in the company of Gonzalo de Sandoval to conquer, restore peace and to establish settlements in the region of Veracruz and Coatzacoalcos?"

"I believe this to be so, for I saw him leave with Captain Sandoval and I afterwards heard it said that he went with him to those regions."

"Do you know if the said Bernal Díaz went with Rodrigo Rangel to conquer and bring peace to the provinces of Copilco and Amatan when the natives had risen against His Majesty?"

"I testify to this being the truth and that Bernal Díaz did all he could to serve His Majesty and that for these services, he and the other conquerors have not received their just reward."

With this last question answered, Cristóbal Hernández reaffirmed that his testimony was the truth. He then signed the written declarations, and the notary requested Bernal Díaz to bring his other witnesses two days later.

On February 12, Bernal appeared at the office of the *alcalde* with Martín Vásquez, whom Bernal later described as "very rich and prominent"; Bartolomé de Villanueva, who had been on the expedition to Honduras; and one Miguel Sánchez de Gascón, also a companion on the expedition and a neighbor of Bernal Díaz in the town of Espíritu Santo. All three gave testimony similar to that of Cristóbal Hernández, although Villanueva revealed some new details as far as the Honduras expedition was concerned.[9]

When asked if it were true Bernal Díaz took part in it and sustained many hardships, Villanueva answered: "I affirm it to be so because I was present on this expedition and we all suffered from hunger and great thirst. It was at this time too, that the horse of Bernal Díaz died and the soldiers were so hungry they ate the meat of it. . . . Besides they never paid him for the horse after they ate it."

The notary also inquired of Villanueva if he was aware "that Báltasar de Osorio, captain of the province of Tabasco, dispossessed Bernal Díaz and took by force the town of Tlapa which had been given Bernal Díaz in *encomienda?*"

Villanueva replied: "I know this to be a fact for I was a witness to it and this was done without Bernal Díaz' being guilty of any crime nor was there any other reason why his land should be taken away from him, except that the borders of the province of Tabasco were being extended. Previous to this I was acquainted with Bernal Díaz for many years and know him to have a good reputation and as leading an honorable life as a Christian."

The words "took . . . by force" cannot be accepted literally. Neither at this hearing nor in such documents as are available is there any evidence that land was seized from Bernal Díaz by force, and it is most unlikely that the old conqueror would have

[9] Cabañas, III, 323.

allowed such property to be taken from him if he were present. What probably happened was that he had not established residence in the towns in his possession and that deeds to the land were transferred to others who were friendly with the governor of the province or with members of the *Audiencia*. At all times the *Audiencia* had the power and the privilege to confiscate land and Indians. This was a common occurrence, one which the conquerors often complained of and used in their arguments that all *encomiendas* should be granted in perpetuity.

Bernal Díaz apparently was not the only one who had trouble with Báltasar de Osorio. On another occasion, when Osorio went to represent Francisco de Montejo before the *Audiencia* in Mexico City, he succeeded in obtaining Montejo's removal as *alcalde mayor* of Tabasco and his own reappointment to that office. He then confiscated all of Montejo's holdings and property in Tabasco, including his *encomiendas* and *haciendas*. But Osorio was far from being the only man to seize land, as the next question put to Bernal's witness indicated.

Villanueva was asked: "Do you know that when Captain Mazariegos went to establish settlements in Chiapas, he dispossessed and took by force from Bernal Díaz the town of Chamula and the adjoining land and made it part of Chiapas?"

To this Villanueva responded: "I affirm it to be so and that the town and land were seized from Bernal Díaz without good reason, except that the province of Chiapas was being populated. The land was taken by force and against the will of Bernal Díaz, who, to my knowledge, has not been compensated for his losses."

"On this matter, do you know if Bernal Díaz filed legal action in Coatzacoalcos over these towns and others and that he has failed to obtain any redress for the losses and damages he suffered?"

84

"Yes, for it is well known that Bernal Díaz, because of these circumstances, is poor and in great need and without funds to press further his legal suits and without any possibility of recovering what was unlawfully seized from him." Then Villanueva could not help putting in a word for himself: "Bernal Díaz has suffered many hardships as I and others who have served His Majesty, and none of us have ever been justly rewarded for these services and we are all of us starving."

This last statement is of course an exaggeration. Some of the conquerors, through luck and opportunity, fared better than others and received land and Indians of greater value, but no one went hungry after the Conquest, and it would be hard to believe that either Villanueva or Bernal ever missed a meal because of their financial condition.

To the question of whether Bernal Díaz was an honorable person of excellent reputation and of some fame as a conversationalist, Villanueva declared that it was true and that Bernal had acted as *procurador* of Espíritu Santo and then as *regidor,* a position he still held.

The final question put to Villanueva was: "Is it true that the said Bernal Díaz has never received compensation for the said towns taken from him in the provinces of Tabasco and Chiapas and that though he has gone many times before the President of the *Audiencia* and before the Viceroy, they have always told him they cannot grant him new *encomiendas* without an order from His Majesty? Tell all you know of this."

"I know this to be so," Villanueva replied, "and that Bernal Díaz has asked for *encomiendas* from the President of the *Audiencia* as well as from His Excellency, the Viceroy, and that both have turned down his requests. I am also a witness to the fact of how hard Bernal Díaz labored during the Conquest and after it, and how he is now exhausted of energies and is poor."

When the testimony of Villanueva and the other witnesses had been completed, the hearing was again continued for two days.

On the fourteenth of February, Bernal brought before the notary another old friend, Captain Luis Marín, whom he describes as bowlegged, but robust and of good stature, with a russet beard and a face marked with smallpox scars. The former conqueror testified to the first series of questions in the same vein as the other witnesses, though more briefly.[10] He said that he had been acquainted with Bernal Díaz for at least eighteen years and that Bernal had participated in the Conquest and had served as a soldier without pay.

Marín was then asked: "Do you know if Bernal Díaz went with Captain Luis Marín to conquer and to pacify the province of Chiapas, where the natives of this region declared war and had to be subdued and pacified?"

"I know this to be a fact," Marín answered, "because I am the same Luis Marín mentioned in the question, and I was the captain of the said expeditions and Bernal served well under me and in the name of His Majesty, he assisted in the conquest of these provinces, where he proved himself and deserves to be rewarded."

Marín also declared that he knew Bernal had lost various of his *encomiendas* without just reason and that although he had made every effort to be compensated for his losses, nothing had come of it. On the final question Marín testified on behalf of Bernal as follows: "I believe Bernal Díaz is in necessity and has received very little help for the services he has rendered to His Majesty."

[10] *Ibid.,* 330.

After the testimony of Marín, his last witness, had been transcribed, copies of the proceedings were made and given to Bernal.[11]

With his *probanza* completed and certified copies in his hands, Bernal next went to the palace of the *Audiencia* and after a wait of several days managed to see Don Antonio de Mendoza. Although Mendoza was one of the most capable and kindly viceroys the king ever sent to New Spain, he was one of the busiest men in the country. It was no easy matter to talk to him, and when Bernal eventually did, the interview was brief and to the point.

Bernal wanted profitable land and Indians to work it. The *Audiencia* and Mendoza himself had told him on a previous occasion that they could do nothing for him. The authorization would have to come from Spain. Bernal must have explained during this interview that he was taking Mendoza's advice and would place his case before the king and the Council of the Indies. Would His Lordship, Don Antonio, give him an official letter that might help to open doors for him? After all, he was one of the first conquerors and had served His Majesty well, and he was only asking for what he deserved. He was poor and in great need and he had a common-law wife and two daughters to support.

The viceroy had heard the same story from hundreds of other conquerors and their pleas were always for more land and Indians. None of them, as far as he could find out, were as poverty stricken as they pretended. Yet as he listened to Bernal's

[11] It is to be noted that in these hearings none of the witnesses testified or mentioned that Bernal Díaz participated in the Grijalva expedition to Yucatán. Cabañas points this out, but he also adds that Bernal's son, Francisco Díaz del Castillo, in his own *probanza,* maintained that his father was a member of the expedition. *Ibid.,* 333–34.

story he must have been impressed by the latter's sincerity, for he consented to write a letter on Bernal's behalf.

He called in a secretary and under the date of February 30, 1539,[12] dictated the following letter addressed to Cardinal Siguenza, president of the Council of the Indies, and the other members of the council:

> Very Illustrious and Very Reverend and Very Magnificent Sirs: Bernal Díaz, resident of the province of Coatzacoalcos is leaving to entreat His Majesty to extend to him such royal favors as he can obtain and in compensation for his services in these parts during the discovery, conquest and establishment of peace in this land, and because they have taken from him certain villages which he had in *encomienda,* and which it is said, was done in order to populate the provinces of Chiapas and Tabasco. As he is a deserving person and has served well His Majesty in these parts, I ask that some consideration be given to his case . . . . Very Illustrious and Very Reverend Sirs, I kiss your hands. . . .[13]
>
> *Antonio de Mendoza*

While this was not a forceful letter, it at least had the viceroy's signature and the official seal. If Mendoza could only have mentioned a little more about him, if he could only have made more definite recommendations. But what can an ordinary soldier ask of the king's representative? Satisfied or not, Bernal gladly accepted the letter, thanked Mendoza, and went on his way.

The same day, Bernal went to see Cortés, who was then in Mexico City, and received from him the following letter:

[12] The Gregorian calendar, which we use today, was not adopted until 1582, when Bernal Díaz was a *regidor* in Guatemala. Hence the date February 30.

[13] Cabañas, III, 311.

88

Illustrious, Very Reverend Sir, Most Illustrious Sir and Very Magnificent Sirs:

As I have great obligation to the persons who came with me to win these lands and as this is known to His Majesty, he would be served and his royal conscience eased, if these matters were recalled to him. The bearer of this letter, Bernal Díaz, is one of those who served well in the conquest of this city and also in the expeditions made to Honduras, Guatemala and many other provinces; and above all, he was one of those who came with Francisco de Córdoba, the first discoverer of this land. In all of this Bernal Díaz has labored and served well, of which facts I am a good witness. When he had two towns in the province of Coatzacoalcos and after the country was governed by the royal treasurer, Alonso de Estrada, these towns were taken from him and never have others been given in compensation.

As a consequence, he and his children have had many difficulties and have been in need and in want. It has hurt me to see what has happened to him and in accordance, I wish to inform your lordships of this, not only so you will know of it, but also, as I have said, to relieve His Majesty's royal conscience by helping him. As will be seen from the written account of his services he is taking with him, he is deserving of Your Lordships' favor. In addition to doing it in the name of our emperor, I would be greatly pleased for all which can be done in his behalf.

May God protect and look after your Very Illustrious and Very Reverend life. The true servant of Your Lordship.[14]

The Marqués del Valle.

After Cortés signed the letter and handed it to Bernal, as was the custom, he embraced him and wished him good luck.

Either Bernal borrowed money from Cortés at this time or he may have raised some among friends. He needed all he could

[14] *Ibid.*, 311–12.

get to buy clothes befitting a returning conqueror and to pay for his passage and his stay in Spain. But there was no real urgency, for he had not received the authorization giving him license to proceed to Spain.

From the end of February, he waited for his permit to depart. It was long in coming. The Council of the Indies was never keen for conquerors to visit the mother country. Sometime in late June or early July, news did arrive from Spain, but it was not the kind Bernal had expected. Isabella, the empress, had died, and the emperor and all of Spain were in mourning. Bernal had to put away the colorful clothes he had purchased and dress himself in black.[15]

It was not a good sign, but Bernal's gloom disappeared when shortly afterward he received the license for his voyage. When he sailed from the port of Veracruz, he was no longer a young man with a sword, on the eve of adventure and great riches; he was a conqueror going home, but his pockets were almost as empty as when he left Medina del Campo, the city of his birth.

---

[15] The Empress Isabella died in May, 1539, but the news would not have reached Mexico for at least six weeks.

8 ♪ *THE RETURN*
OF A CONQUEROR

For Bernal Díaz and the other passengers aboard ship, the trip to Spain was not an easy one. The length of a voyage, depending on the weather, varied from five to seven long weeks. The usual route was from Veracruz to Cuba, then through the dangerous Bahama Channel and northeastward between the Virginia Capes and Bermuda until a prevailing northerly wind was picked up at about thirty-eight degrees north latitude, and from there eastward to the Azores. Ships were forbidden to call at other ports before reaching Sanlúcar de Barrameda in Spain.

Atlantic ships in the middle of the sixteenth century were small and usually did not exceed two hundred tons, since vessels of greater tonnage could not clear the bar at Sanlúcar without unloading. A one-hundred-ton ship was allowed to carry thirty passengers, though many times this restriction was evaded by signing up additional passengers as crew members. The captain was often the owner of the ship, and he always had with him a pilot who was both first mate and navigator. The sea charts were crude, although remarkably accurate considering the few instruments available. The vessels were quite seaworthy, even if their wooden hulls leaked and there was so much bilge water the passengers frequently had to go barefoot.[1]

Life at sea was not pleasant. There were no sleeping quarters except for the captain; the sailors and soldiers lay on the deck or in any place they could find room. A few brought on board small, hard mattresses and blankets of goatskin, but Bernal Díaz was not one of them. By now he had become accustomed to sleeping on the floor, a habit he continued long after the Conquest. He disregarded the idea of a hammock, which the Spaniards had found the Indians using in their huts and which were soon adopted by ships of all nations. There were no bathroom facilities. The public privy, called a *jardín* ("the garden"), was a seat hung over the rail forward or aft. It is said that when a man of the Church used it, the sailors and others turned their heads.

"The ship is like a jail and suffocatingly close from the heat," Fray Tomás de la Torre reported in his journal, adding that "most everyone sleeps on the floor, though there are a few who have brought with them mattresses made of dog's hair. . . . No one has any desire to eat and there is an incredible thirst from the hardtack and the salted food. . . . The drinking water is rationed and only those who bring their own wine have any to drink. . . . The lice eat one alive and the smells below deck from the bilge water are intolerable."[2]

Each passenger was expected to travel armed and to provide his own food, which usually consisted of hardtack, wine, drinking water, and water for washing and shaving. We can be certain that when Bernal Díaz sailed, he provided well for himself,

[1] Samuel Eliot Morison, *Admiral of the Ocean Sea,* 183–96. See chap. XII for interesting details on shipping and navigation of the time.

[2] Fray Tomás de la Torre, *Desde Salamanca, España, hasta Ciudad Real, Chiapas, diario de viaje, 1544–45,* 72, 86.

taking with him an extra ration of *bizcochos,* the hardtack of the period, a slab of bacon, and a bundle of *tasajos,* beef dried in the sun and salted. He must have brought with him several *botijas* of wine, for as he said, "thirst knows no law." They sailed on dead reckoning, which meant setting a course by the compass and estimating distances traveled on a chart. As in all ships of that time, the few aids to navigation consisted of a mariner's compass, a divider, quadrants and a lead line, a traverse table, an ordinary multiplication table, and an astronomer's ephemeris. The exact time of day, so important in calculating the daily position of ships at sea, was kept by a sand clock, a half-hour glass in most cases. They also used the North Star, but since they did not know how to apply the proper corrections, it was not always helpful.

We do not know on what ship or on what date Bernal sailed from Veracruz, for he did not mention it in his history or in any of his letters. He did write, however, that he left two months before Cortés, which would be about January, 1540. We know definitely that Bernal was in Spain in April of that year, waiting for an audience with the Council of the Indies.

Bernal does not describe what happened to him in Spain; either his experiences there were too painful or he did not believe them of sufficient interest to be included in his story of the Conquest. There are no letters, no notes of any kind, which might fill in the gaps during his stay. If he went to visit his mother and father and brother, as would seem likely, he does not refer to it. Even for his appearance before the Council of the Indies we must draw on material from other documents and sources. Bernal Díaz kept to himself everything which happened to him in Spain, and he had good reason for doing so. Only in one or two paragraphs does he touch upon his visit.

"When I went to Castile and on arrival there, I changed into

93

mourning, as was required, because of the death of Our Queen, Our Lady," he wrote. "And in this period, there came to the court from Peru, Hernando Pizarro with more than forty men all in heavy mourning and Cortés and his servants, also in black."[3] Then he adds: "There were so many of us in Spain at this time on matters of business, that they jokingly referred to us as 'Peruvian Indians in mourning.' "

But Bernal's visit to Spain was far from a jesting matter. For if he had hoped for the glories and honors of a returning conqueror, he was disappointed. Conquerors in Spain were by this time commonplace, and no one thought of them as heroes; talk of their adventures was no longer of much interest.

Despite his letters from Cortés and the viceroy, Bernal was having a difficult time getting a hearing from the Council of the Indies. They kept him waiting for days and then refused to read his documents, referring him instead to the *fiscal,* the king's attorney, at Valladolid.

All petitions, he was informed, had to pass through the usual official channels and had to have the approval of the *fiscal* before they could be acted upon. Bernal evidently did not lose his temper or his confidence at all this governmental red tape, but immediately presented his documents to the *fiscal.* The reason for what happened there is beyond even the wildest guess, for the *fiscal, Licenciado* Don Juan de Villalobos, refused to recognize Bernal's claims or accept the fact that he was a conqueror.[4]

Later, when the Council of the Indies investigated the matter, they reported: "When he [Bernal Díaz] went before our *fiscal,*

---

[3] Hernando Pizarro, on his return to Spain in 1540, was imprisoned for twenty years for the murder of Diego de Almagro in Peru. See William H. Prescott, *History of the Conquest of Peru,* 1065.

[4] Genaro García (ed.), *Historia verdadera de la conquista de la Nueva España, por Bernal Díaz del Castillo,* I, xiiff.

Licenciado Villalobos, we were told that we should not heed his petition or grant him any favors as requested by the said Bernal Díaz, because he was never a conqueror, as he claimed, and he never had in *encomienda* such towns as he maintained were taken from him."[5] Somewhere there must have been a grave confusion of identities.

Bernal Díaz originally left Spain in 1514, but there is no official record of his shipping out on that date. Justo Zaragoza, who edited the history of Bernal's great-great-grandson, Antonio Francisco Fuentes y Guzmán, explains the action of the *fiscal* by stating that in the register of the Casa de Contratación in Seville, of those who went to New Spain between 1509 and 1517, there appears the name of "Alonso Díaz, son of Bernal Díaz, citizen of Toledo." This obviously refers to another Bernal Díaz, a name quite common in Spain. However, Zaragoza points out: "The *fiscal* confused the hero of Chamula [Bernal Díaz] with the father of that passenger, who might perhaps have asked some grant for the services of his son."[6] In spite of this explanation, it seems inconceivable that the *fiscal* should reject as false the letters of Cortés and Viceroy Mendoza and the documentary evidence in the *probanza*. Yet he did just that.

We can readily picture how Bernal must have felt to be told to his face that he was not a conqueror!

As Bernal walked the streets of Valladolid, his documents in a leather purse hanging from his shoulder, he must have been brokenhearted. He was extremely sensitive and was not prepared for such a shock. He, not a conqueror? Had he heard right?

Perhaps at a *mesón* where he ordered a glass of jerez or on a

[5] *Ibid.*
[6] *Ibid.*

bench in the plaza facing the cathedral, he opened his leather case and examined again the documents he had brought with him: the letters signed by Cortés and Mendoza, the testimony of Villanueva and Hernández and Vásquez and Luis Marín. How could anyone question their authenticity? Were they not proof enough? How could the *fiscal* say he was not Bernal Díaz? He carefully folded his papers and put them away, too deeply hurt to understand what had happened to him.

Bernal Díaz must have felt both humiliated and angry—and with reason. He well might have asked himself why he had ever returned to Spain, why he had gone through all the privations and dangers in Mexico and Honduras. Was this the way the king rewarded his soldiers? That he, Bernal Díaz del Castillo, veteran of 119 battles, should be called a liar! The ignominy of it was too much to accept, even for such a stouthearted soldier as Bernal Díaz.

If he was not a conqueror, then what had he been doing in Mexico? Who had fought side by side with Cortés, Sandoval, and Alvarado? Who had helped to seize the mighty Montezuma? Who had gone through the jungles of Petén and Honduras? Who had found food for the soldiers and the officers when they were starving?

We do not know what Bernal did after his unfortunate encounter with the *fiscal*, but we cannot be far wrong in assuming that he did what was his usual custom when in difficulties. He probably went to the cathedral, a short distance from the building where the *fiscal* had his offices, and there prayed to "Our Lord Jesus Christ and His Blessed Mother who has always guided me and given me strength."

"The *fiscal* humiliated Bernal doubly," writes Genaro García, the Mexican historian, "for not only did he refuse to recognize his services during so many years of hardships and dangers, but he treated him as if he had falsified his documents, and this to Bernal who always proclaimed the truth as sacred. This abuse on the part of the *fiscal*, without doubt, hurt Bernal more than anything else which had happened to him."[7]

But Bernal could not be defeated that easily. Once the shock was over, he faced the challenge squarely. He would prove to them that a grave mistake had been made. How could anyone be the least dubious of who he was and what he had done? He would take his case right back to the Council of the Indies, and he would not leave Spain until he was completely vindicated and justly compensated.

Bernal Díaz now sought an audience with the Council of the Indies. He needed all his patience and persistence, for justice came from the council slowly and with great reluctance—when it came at all. While he never described his own predicament, he did record what happened to one of his acquaintances, Miguel Díaz de Auz, during this period. This man, a captain in the fleet of Francisco de Garay, unable to get satisfaction from the council and after making a series of accusations before the members, "threw his cape on the floor," Bernal related, "and dropping to his knees, placed a dagger over his heart and cried out: 'If what I say is not true, Your Highnesses, then kill me with this dagger. But if what I say is the truth, then let justice be done.' " Bernal, who was a witness to this scene, added that the president of the council "ordered the supplicant to rise and declared they were not there to destroy anyone, but to administer justice to the deserving."

This scene must have taken place some months after Bernal's

[7] *Bernal Díaz del Castillo: noticias bio-bibliográficas,* p. 29.

own appearance before the council in April of 1540. The council was presided over at the time by Fray García de Loaisa, archbishop of Seville, and among the members was a man named Bernal Díaz de Luco, who, unfortunately, was not related to the petitioner. Early in April, after listening to Bernal's account of his experience with the *fiscal* and after reading the documents presented, including the *probanza,* the council firmly sustained Bernal's standing as a conqueror and recognized the losses of the towns he held in *encomienda.* In accordance with their decision, they issued a *cédula:*

> On examining the various petitions and documents, the members of the Council of the Indies, in the name of His Majesty, decree and order that a royal *cédula* be sent to the Viceroy in New Spain so that he will be informed of the quality and quantity of the towns which were granted to the said Bernal Díaz and which were taken from him . . . and that other towns of equal value be given to him in the same province and in compensation for his losses . . . .[8]

Certain provisions of the *cédula* still did not satisfy Bernal, and shortly afterward he again went to the council, this time with a petition in which he maintained that the orders could not be carried out, for all the towns in the provinces of Chiapas and Tabasco had already been distributed to the other conquerors and there would be none available for himself. He asked instead *encomiendas* in other parts of New Spain, or in the province of Guatemala, where land and Indians were still available.

During the period of his appearance before the Council of the Indies, word of the arrival of Cortés in Spain reached Bernal. He saw his former commander for the last time in Madrid, and

[8] Cabañas, III, 305.

it is quite possible that Cortés helped him, with what little influence he had left, to obtain the three additional *cédulas* granted to Bernal in June and July of 1540. The first of these, directed to Pedro de Alvarado, governor of Guatemala, read in part:

I the King. To *Adelantado* Don Pedro de Alvarado, our governor of the province of Guatemala and to our deputies to each one of you, to whom this *cédula* is manifested: Bernal Díaz, resident of the town of Espíritu Santo has informed me that he is one of the first conquerors of New Spain, having spent there more than twenty-five years when he went with Francisco Hernández de Córdoba and later in the company of Don Hernán Cortés, Marqués del Valle, on which occasions he bore arms and assisted in the discovery, the conquest and bringing peace to New Spain. As the result of these campaigns, he suffered many hardships, much hunger, and great privations and in compensation for his services, the governors of this land gave him in *repartimiento* and in *encomienda,* the towns of Chamula, Micapa and Tlapa which are in the provinces of Chiapas and Tabasco; having them in his possession he administered them and enjoyed their income and tributes. Subsequently these towns were taken from him as evidenced by the documents he presented to our Council of the Indies, and while this was done in our service, until now, he has received no compensation for his losses.

In view of his being one of the first conquerors and discoverers of New Spain and having two young daughters, and having great necessity, he has entreated us that we give him other towns in New Spain of equal value in income as those previously held. . . . As it is our wish and desire that the said Bernal Díaz be given just compensation in the province of Guatemala, even though the towns taken from him were not in that province, we order you to assign to him in accordance with our *cédula* such Indians as are available, and if not to give him the first which are available. Dated at Madrid this nineteenth day of June, 1540.

Fray García, Cardinal Hispalensis, By order of His Majesty and by the governor in his name.[9]

Juan de Sámano.

After the Conquest, Pedro de Alvarado had gone on to Guatemala, where he had established a settlement and had then been named *adelantado* and governor of the province. Bernal still considered himself a friend of Alvarado's, and naturally he would have expected the governor to look after him. Yet there must have been some misgivings in Bernal's heart about Alvarado, or perhaps Cortés said to him: "Look here, Bernal Díaz, see to it that Alvarado is forced to carry out this order. If not, he may not heed it. Old friends are often forgotten." Whether the decision to do so came from Cortés' advice or was simply his own prudent idea, Bernal managed another *cédula* from the royal council. This document, addressed to the *audiencia* in the province of Guatemala, clearly conveys some of Bernal's doubts of old friendship caught up in politics:

I the King. To *Licenciado* Cerrato, our president of the *Real Audiencia de los Confines*. As ye well know and as I have ordered and given two *cédulas* which are as follows: [The *cédulas* addressed to Alvarado and to Viceroy Mendoza are here repeated.]

And as the said Bernal Díaz has informed us that our governor in the province of Guatemala may protest and refuse to comply with our instructions in the said *cédulas,* because he may want to reward his friends or other persons, and as the said Bernal Díaz would suffer great difficulties if the favors requested were not granted him, he has asked us to see that our *cédulas* be enforced without obstacles or delays and so it is my wish . . . and if the said governor

[9] *Ibid.,* 304.

of the said province of Guatemala does not comply with our *cédulas,* we command ye to see that it be done and that the said Bernal Díaz shall not suffer injury or delay . . . .[10]

The last *cédula* which Bernal Díaz received while in Spain was dated July 2, 1540, and was addressed to Don Antonio de Mendoza, the viceroy of New Spain and president of the *Real Audiencia.* This *cédula* was similar in content and instructions to the previous ones and ordered that Bernal be allowed just compensation for the towns he had lost. The council also requested that Bernal be granted an official post in Micapa, Suchititan, or Soconusco, "which are near where he is settled or in the towns near Guatemala where he will wait for the said compensation to be rendered."[11] The council apparently felt there would be some delay before Bernal was given new towns, for in urging that he be named to an official position, the *cédula* stressed that he "cannot support his house and children and is in great financial need."[12]

While these *cédulas* were issued to Bernal in the king's name, this was merely a customary procedure and nowhere is there a suggestion that the king ever saw him or was even aware of his existence. Bernal speaks of going to the court and of seeing there Cortés and Hernando Pizarro, but this is mentioned so casually that such a visit is highly questionable. If he had been presented to the king, Bernal would have made the most of it. As a matter of fact, during this period, Charles V was in Flanders.

In view of his treatment and what he actually received, Bernal was not as successful as he expected, and he must have been dis-

---

[10] *Ibid.,* 306.
[11] *Ibid.,* 307.
[12] *Ibid.,* 308.

appointed with the results of his trip to Spain. Although he did get some recognition from the Council of the Indies, what they granted him was little enough. They affirmed that he was a conqueror and had been with Córdoba and Cortés; they acknowledged that he had suffered unusual hardships and had served his country and the king well; they agreed that vassals in his possession had been taken away from him and that he should be compensated for his losses, and they commanded that this be done. But the council gave him no more than he had had originally.

When he sailed from Mexico, he had convinced himself that he would be amply rewarded. He had been hopeful of an audience with the king, and perhaps he had even dreamed of winning powerful friends in court, of meeting people of importance, which might have led to a successful marriage and a rich dowry. Instead he had been confronted with the *fiscal,* who accused him of not being a conqueror; he had spent his time and what little money he had in proving his case and getting promises of future compensations. The royal *cédulas* in his leather purse were valuable, but only if they were carried out. And Bernal had been in New Spain long enough to know what often happened when *cédulas* were presented.

During his disheartening stay in Spain he saw that at least he was not the only one who failed to get satisfaction. Even the great Cortés had been turned down; none of the gold he had sought in payment for his expeditions was forthcoming. At this time, too, Hernando Pizarro was attempting to defend himself against the serious charges which had been preferred against him, and as Bernal Díaz tells us, "they put Hernando Pizarro in prison in the Mota at Medina." Bernal remembered well that prison fortress in his home town of Medina del Campo, and his childhood memories of it must have made him vividly aware of the plight of returning conquerors. He arranged passage as quickly as he could and was glad to embark for Mexico.

When he sailed from Spain, Bernal was forty-five years old. The most exciting part of his life was over, the most important part just beginning. It would be enlightening if he had jotted down his thoughts at the time. Was he still embittered at the treatment he had received in Spain? If so, it does not show in any of his letters or in his work. Sometimes he complained and criticized, but never is there any sign of his being vituperative or vengeful.

Had he turned over in his mind the possibility of writing his history? It is probable that, in view of what occurred to him and to others in Spain, the idea of preparing an account of the Conquest from the soldier's point of view began to formulate during those long, quiet days aboard ship on the return voyage. Bernal might also have carried back with him a volume of Cortés' letters, which had been published between 1522 and 1526. If he did, the reading of these letters must have irked him and convinced him further of the need for telling the story of the Conquest as he saw it.

He was furious at Cortés for taking most of the credit for the success of the expedition and not sharing it with his men. Bernal felt that had Cortés done so, he, Bernal Díaz, and his companions would have gained greater recognition and financial reward. "He made no effort to recall our valiant deeds," Bernal lamented. "God forgive him for his sins."

Ramón Iglesia says that if Las Casas championed the rights of the Indians, Bernal Díaz defended the rights of the conquerors.[13]

[13] "Two Articles on the Same Topic," *Hispanic American Historical Review*, Vol. XX (1940), 517-50.

Bernal did for his companions and for himself what no other historian had done and what Cortés had failed to do in his otherwise brilliant letters to the king.

As the ship on which he was traveling left Spain, Bernal Díaz could not perceive that the fame he so much sought would someday come to him. At the moment, he must only have looked forward to the friendly shores of the land he had helped to conquer. So far away from Spain, this land was nevertheless where he belonged. He was going home.

9   *LAND GRANTS AND A WIFE WITH A DOWRY*

B ERNAL DÍAZ had not seen Pedro de Alvarado since the Honduras expedition, when they had traveled together from Guatemala to Mexico. In that interval of some fourteen years, Alvarado had been raised to the rank of *adelantado* and had gone with a fleet of vessels toward Peru to try for his share of the spoils.[1] But because of the trouble he might cause, the lieutenants of Pizarro had bought him off in Ecuador with a payment of silver bars totaling one hundred thousand gold castellanos. This seemed a sizable sum—until Alvarado found on his return that the silver had been mixed with copper.

When Bernal Díaz arrived in Veracruz from Spain in 1540, Pedro de Alvarado was preparing another expedition, this time to the South Seas and the Spice Islands. For this project he invested all his money and what he could borrow. Bernal later

---

[1] Alvarado did not get to Peru, but only as far as Ecuador, where his fleet and armaments were bought by Almagro and Belalcázar. See. Bancroft, *op. cit.,* II, 129.

learned that Alvarado's expenses were enormous. "He spent so much that neither the wealth he brought from Peru, nor what he obtained from the mines, nor the tributes from his towns, nor what was lent him by his friends and relatives, was enough," Bernal says, without mentioning that the Peruvian riches had been reduced by the copper content of the silver.

Alvarado, then governor of Guatemala, left his wife, Beatriz de la Cueva, in the capital and commissioned her cousin, Francisco de la Cueva, to act as lieutenant governor. Before the expedition was under way, Alvarado was called to suppress a revolt of the natives in the province of Jalisco. He was seriously injured when a falling horse crushed him, and he died in Guadalajara.[2] Word of his death quickly spread throughout Mexico, and before long, Bernal Díaz heard of it.

Bernal found himself in a predicament he had not anticipated. Of the three royal *cédulas* granted to him in Spain, the most important one was directed to Pedro de Alvarado. Bernal's future depended on this *cédula*. Now, with Alvarado dead, it seemed worthless, for although it was addressed to Alvarado and his deputies, his deputies could mean anyone.

Slowly Bernal began to realize that his situation was more hopeless than before. His trip to Spain had been something of a disappointment, and yet there had always been a chance that Alvarado would let him choose some really good land and towns. For the moment, even that chance faded away.

The news from Guatemala was not encouraging either. When Mendoza officially informed the *cabildo* of Guatemala of the governor's fate, Alvarado's wife, Doña Beatriz, became hysterical from grief. In a Latin outburst of emotion she is reported to have beaten her face, torn her hair, and to have screamed blas-

[2] *Ibid.,* 207.

phemously. Her house was stained black inside and out, and the cathedral was draped in mourning.[3]

Doña Beatriz, however, recovered sufficiently from her sorrow to accept Mendoza's appointment and become the first woman governor in the New World. As Alvarado's widow, Bernal felt, she might well honor his *cédulas*. He could appeal to her, he could describe his long friendship with her husband, and perhaps in the end he could get more from her than he could have obtained from Alvarado.

In September of 1541, with this thought in mind, Bernal made plans for moving to Guatemala. He hoped to be there at least by the early part of the following year. His *cédula* to Mendoza had obviously not received much consideration, or he would not have decided to leave Mexico. He had been certain, even while in Spain, that his best opportunity for good land and Indians was in Guatemala: the province was large enough and the conquerors who had settled there were few in number. He remembered the country well from when he passed through it on his return from Honduras.

Just as Bernal was getting ready for his departure, again there came news, more dramatic and disturbing than the death of Alvarado. Either from an earthquake or from excessive rains which had fallen during the rainy season, the rising waters in the crater of the Volcán de Agua, situated on the edge of the capital of Guatemala, broke through. The water rushed down the ten-thousand-foot height with tremendous force and struck the city in the early hours of the evening. The disaster was so swift and so unexpected that many were drowned before they knew what had happened. Neither Spaniards nor Indians were spared; the death toll was one hundred Spaniards and six hun-

[3] Dorothy H. Popenoe, *Santiago de los Caballeros de Guatemala*, 21.

dred Indians. Among those who died were Doña Beatriz and her ladies in waiting. One of the few survivors in her household was Doña Leonor, the daughter of Pedro de Alvarado by the Indian princess given to him years before at Tlaxcala in the presence of Bernal Díaz.

When word of this catastrophe reached Bernal, he must have seriously wondered if he was fated ever to live in Guatemala. The death of Alvarado and his widow and the destruction of the city were all bad omens. Would it not be wiser to remain in Mexico and be satisfied with the little he had?

He hastily brushed aside such gloomy thoughts. True, it would be easier if Pedro de Alvarado were alive. He could talk to him, recall their experiences and privations together, and plead with him as a friend. Now there was no Alvarado from whom to ask favors, only a new governor. Alonso de Maldonado, late *oidor* of the *Audiencia* of Mexico. Before him, a virtual stranger, he, Bernal Díaz del Castillo, would have to appear. But to an adventurer in search of security, new pastures always looked more promising, and Guatemala still seemed to Bernal the best place to live quietly and well for the rest of his life.

Having made his decision, Bernal proceeded to settle his affairs. He had at this time two daughters by a native woman, about whom little is known. To the one named Teresa he assigned his *encomienda* of Indians in Coatzacoalcos, while the other daughter either went with him or joined him later.[4]

Bernal makes no mention of his trip to Guatemala, although it marked the beginning of a new life for him. If there was a lump in his throat as he started on his journey, it was not from bitterness but from the fact that he was leaving Mexico. It was

[4] Tejada to Mondéjar, in Francisco del Paso y Troncoso (ed.), *Epistolario de Nueva España, 1505–1818*, VI, 35–36.

not easy for him to depart from a land he had helped to conquer and to colonize. He would never forget Mexico, with its vast valleys and high plateaus, its icy winds that swept down from Popocatepetl, and the hot, humid weather of his own province of Coatzacoalcos. He would miss the people of Mexico, too, and the last embrace with old friends he would not see again was painful. Once more he would be alone and on his own. He had very little to take with him except the royal *cédulas,* which he now carried in the leather pouch hanging on straps from his shoulder. So far, these *cédulas* had not gained him anything, but perhaps he would have better luck with them in Guatemala.

The trip was long and weary, though he traveled over the newly opened route through the Cuchumatanes Mountains by way of Todos Santos. From there he went on to Chiantla and then across the Quiché highlands to Chichicastenango and again through more mountain country until he finally reached the valley of Panchoy, where the present city of Antigua is located.

When he looked down upon the city which was to be his future home, he was pleasantly surprised. The new site for the town had only recently been chosen, but already men were at work and new homes were going up. The church was almost completed, the streets and the plaza had been laid out. The climate was refreshingly cool and the air dry. Then, as his eyes scanned the landscape, he saw, quite close, the three volcanoes, one smoking, the other scarred from where the water had come rushing out, and the third hiding between the two. They looked threatening, and for a moment Bernal recalled the earthquakes this land had had when he passed through it years before. But what mattered tremors of the earth to one who had been a conqueror? He dug his heels into his horse, yelled at his servants on foot to follow him, and began the descent.

Bernal Díaz arrived in Santiago de los Caballeros at just the

right time: the population had not fully recovered from the disaster; there was still a great deal of fear and confusion. Many
settlers, convinced that another volcanic eruption would follow,
had fled from Guatemala and established themselves in Honduras, Nicaragua, and Costa Rica. Others, despite the assurance
of Bishop Marroquín that God was not punishing the capital for
the blasphemies of Doña Beatriz, had taken to fervent prayers
and to religious processions and demonstrations.

Alonso de Maldonado, the acting governor of the province,
seemed to Bernal Díaz to be capable and fair. Anxious to set at
ease the fears of the people and to establish new confidence in
his government, Maldonado had need for men such as Bernal
Díaz and he welcomed Bernal as a future resident with more
warmth than he might have shown at some other period.

When Bernal presented the *cédulas* he had obtained from the
Council of the Indies, Governor Maldonado treated them with
respect and consideration. As Bernal had suspected, there was
still a large amount of land and Indians available in Guatemala,
and he was assigned three *encomiendas,* which included the
towns of Zacatepec, Joazagazapa, and Mistán. He was promised, in addition, that if these grants did not prove sufficiently
profitable, he would be given others. This was a pleasant change
for Bernal after his cold encounters with government officials.
He was delighted, too, at finding that a number of the settlers
in Guatemala were veteran conquerors like himself. He even
met several old friends who had been with him in the Cortés
expedition to Mexico.

There was talk at this time of his becoming a member of the
cabildo, or municipal council. Because the official records for
this specific period are lost, the exact date when Bernal was appointed to the *cabildo* is not known, but the historian Fray Fran-

cisco Vásquez, who had an opportunity to examine the records while they were extant, wrote that in 1546 and probably before then Bernal Díaz was serving the city as *procurador general,* or what might be called general counsel or city attorney.

Vásquez gives an interesting sidelight on what was happening in the city that year. Just before Easter in 1546, the Franciscan priests, never satisfied with the site selected for the new city, had retired to their old monastery, which was still standing. "The townspeople finding themselves without Franciscan priests and Easter approaching without the hope of sermons, made an appeal to the *cabildo.*"[5] On March 1, the *cabildo* met and decreed "that because the priests of the Order of San Francisco have left the monastery and have gone to Ciudad Vieja, we hereby instruct Alcalde Juan Pérez Dardón, Regidor Hernán Méndez and Procurador Bernal Díaz to request, on the part of God and the King, that the priests return to the monastery because of their great need in this city."[6] The three-man commission then went to near-by Ciudad Vieja to interview the priests and was apparently successful, according to Vásquez, for the priests returned to Santiago in time for the customary Easter services.

One of the minor problems the governor and prelates in the Spanish colonies had from the very beginning was how to induce eligible bachelors holding *encomiendas* to marry. Many of the settlers lived with Indian women, but only a few ever married them. In 1538, before Bernal's arrival in Guatemala, a royal decree had been issued ordering that all *encomenderos* marry within three years from the date of their notification or forfeit

[5] *Crónica de la provincia del santísimo nombre de Jesús de Guatemala,* I, *lib.* i, *cap.* xxiii. See also *cap.* iv.

[6] J. Joaquín Pardo, *Efemerides para escribir la historia de la muy noble y muy leal ciudad de Santiago de los Caballeros del reino de Guatemala,* 10.

their *encomiendas* in favor of married men. This decree was somewhat modified when the Guatemala *cabildo* protested on the grounds that eligible women could be found only in the city of Mexico and that in Guatemala most of the women available were socially inferior.

About this time Bernal Díaz took a native woman as a common-law wife. A document now reposing in the archives in Mexico, written by Bernal's illegitimate son, Diego Díaz del Castillo, states that his mother's name was Angelina and that she was a native woman from Guatemala.[7] In this document, part of a litigation dated 1570, Diego gave his age as twenty-seven, which would indicate that he was born in 1543 and that his father must have taken Angelina as a common-law wife about 1542.

This illegitimate son obviously had the courage of his father. In the litigation in which Diego's name appears, he was brought before the Court of Inquisition in Mexico on charges preferred against him by a priest, Gaspar de Tejada. In the complaint Diego was accused of having instructed his Indians not to attend Mass because the church was too far from his *encomienda*. When faced with these charges, Diego presented to the members of the Inquisition a royal *cédula* he had obtained giving him permission to keep his Indians from attending Mass. The *cédula* was enough to free Diego, and he subsequently sued the priest for the charges made and had him imprisoned.

Illegitimacy was never a cause for not receiving royal favors. The only coat of arms granted to the family of Bernal Díaz was

[7] "Proceso hecho de oficio de la Santa Inquisicíon ordinario contra Diego Díaz del Castillo, natural de Guatemala y hijo de Bernal Díaz del Castillo. 1568," Archivo General de la Nación, Mexico, Inq. Mex. 8.

given, not to his sons born in matrimony, but to Diego Díaz del
Castillo. Either Bernal lived with Diego's mother only a short
time or he kept her as his mistress. He still was not married in
the eyes of the Church, and as the government continued to
frown on landholding Spaniards who did not have legal wives,
Bernal began to look around for a suitable partner, someone
who was not beneath him socially and who could offer at least
the semblance of a dowry.

He found such a person in Teresa Becerra, the only daughter
of Juana de Saavedra and Bartolomé Becerra, one of the conquerors of Guatemala and the first *alacalde ordinario* of the city
of Santiago. Her family was prominent in the colony, and Teresa
was also the widow of Juan Durán, an early settler. While she
must have had certain charms which appealed to Bernal, she
could not have been very young. If she was married the first time
when she was sixteen, and even if she was widowed almost immediately, several years of mourning had to pass before Spanish
custom permitted her to remarry.

The exact date of her marriage to Bernal Díaz is unknown.
All of the *libros de casamientos de españoles* still preserved in the
Cathedral of Guatemala have been examined, but the volume
which would record the marriage was either destroyed or lost,
for those still extant go back only to 1577. However, in the municipal archives there is a document dated May 15, 1544, in
which both Bernal Díaz and Teresa Becerra testified to the royal
notary, Juan de León, that Bernal received a dowry which
totaled 880 pesos.[8] From this document we know that Bernal
was married to Teresa either early that year or in the latter part

---

[8] This may be taken as further evidence that Bernal Díaz came to Guatemala soon after the disaster of 1541.

of the previous year. This is further confirmed in the *probanza* of their first son, Francisco Díaz del Castillo, which he made in 1568 and in which he gave his age as twenty-three.

The dowry consisted of eight hundred pesos in cash and the remaining eighty pesos in clothing material, including three mantles, one of taffeta, the other two of wool, and a sash of blue velvet and one of fine lace and another of silk. If the marriage proved unsuccesful and there was a separation, Bernal agreed to return all he had received to Teresa's father.

A dowry of eight hundred pesos was not a great deal of money in Guatemala, even in those days. It is difficult to interpret the monetary values of that period in present-day terms, but we can make a comparison. As early as 1532, the Guatemala *cabildo,* in order to stop inflation, set fixed prices on what could be charged within the province. For example, a blacksmith charged a *tostón,* or half a peso, for shoeing a horse; a tailor was paid one and one-half pesos for making a wool cape, while the extraction of a horse's tooth cost two pesos. On the other hand, a dozen nails cost half a peso, and one large table knife, if the steel and iron were provided, came to two and one-half pesos. If a Spaniard went to jail, he had to pay half a peso if he was there only during the day, but if he slept inside the jail, the rate went up to one peso daily.

Labor was cheap, as were lumber and such building material as adobe bricks. Since there was no need for such expensive items as plumbing, the construction of a modest house in the middle of the sixteenth century did not cost more than two hundred to four hundred pesos. With the dowry he received, Bernal Díaz could well have put up a house for his wife and perhaps he did just that.

Bernal had every reason to feel pleased and happy. He was married to a daughter of a prominent conqueror who held a high position in the city government, he himself was an official of the *cabildo,* and he possessed three *encomiendas.* The only dark cloud for him and the other settlers in Guatemala was the New Laws of the Indies. The enforcement of these laws threatened the entire way of life of New Spain and its provinces. Bernal now began a long and losing battle against them, a battle which was to take him to Spain for a second time.

10 ♪ *OFFICIAL MISSION TO SPAIN*

BERNAL DÍAZ had a deep respect for the clergy as long as his privileges and those of his fellow settlers were not in jeopardy. During and after the Conquest there had been a harmonious blending of the sword and the Cross. Soldier and priest usually got along well, for their general objectives were the same: to subjugate and to Christianize. Bernal has described in detail their prayers, their confessions, the altars constructed in the wilderness, and the wisdom of Fray Olmedo, who accompanied the expedition of Cortés.

Bernal was somewhat evasive in describing the breach between the padres and the conquerors—a breach which had widened greatly by the time he sat down to write his history—but he could not always hide his rancor against the men of God. He trusted and believed in them, but he could not help seeing that they occasionally violated the trusts bestowed upon them. At first, in the face of danger and uncertainty, the Spanish conquerors had for their own religion simply a blind faith.

In the stone images of the Aztecs the Spaniards saw only cruel and revengeful gods, to be destroyed with the zealous satisfaction of crusading missionaries. Still, in replacing the idols with images of the Madonna and Child, as symbols of tenderness and forgiveness, the conquerors failed to recognize the inconsistency of preaching a gospel of peace through threats and violence.

In the early days there was little genuine conversion of the natives to Christianity, nor could there have been in the space of time allowed. What happened was a forced substitution of images, and because the Indians were deeply religious and superstitious and because the new faith had resemblances to their old religion, they accepted it more easily than can be realized. Not only the priests but even Bernal Díaz was surprised at how fast they took to Mass and prayers, although in reality they did not fully understand what it was they worshiped. As new churches were constructed, natives were baptized and converted by the thousands, without any religious instruction whatsoever. Fray Motolinía wrote that "in five days that I was in that monastery another priest and I baptized by count 15,200," which was not an unusual figure. Two other priests, he testifies, baptized more than 15,000 at Xochimilco in a single day![1]

The Spanish priests burned incense and they created the same kind of magic the Aztec priests had performed. There were no high temples now, but high-domed churches with altars of silver and gold. There were saints for every day and for every occasion. But now no one had to be sacrificed, no one had to give his heart and blood to the gods.

Not all of the conquerors and colonists were deeply religious. We know from the records of the Guatemala *cabildo* that rigid

---

[1] Quoted in Cerwin, *op. cit.,* 298–99.

laws had to be passed in order to force the colonists to attend divine services. Those who failed to go faced three days' imprisonment or a fine of three gold pesos.

From Bernal's pen we hear the clergy praised. "Since we conquered these lands everyone possible has been baptized, including men, women and children who previously would have lost their souls in purgatory," he wrote, "and this has come about because we have so many good Franciscan and Dominican priests.... Another good thing, the natives know the holy prayers in their own language and when they pass an altar or a cross they lower their heads in humility and then kneeling they recite *Pater Noster.*"[2]

There was one group of priests whom Bernal respected and at the same time bitterly opposed. These were the Dominicans, led by Bartolomé de las Casas, who was determined to abolish Indian slavery. They were the liberals and radicals of that period, and their ideology brought upon them both the hatred of the colonists and stiff opposition from the Franciscans. Bancroft writes of this:

> The disagreement between the two highest orders [Franciscans and Dominicans] was not based entirely upon a struggle for supremacy. Each has its distinct views with regard to the method of implanting Christianity in America. The Dominicans . . . would not recognize wholesale baptism as practised by the Franciscans and they would not admit that the interests of the conquerors were compatible with the welfare of the conquered races. The Franciscans, with Motolinía as their leader, imagined that a system of ecclesiastical and civil policy could be adopted which would conduce to the interests of both the dominant and conquered races.

[2] BDC, *cap.* ccix.

118

This order did not object to the sword being called into operation; the Dominicans denied it as a means of advancing the gospel.[3]

As early as 1536, Las Casas had written a treatise advocating peaceful subjugation as the best means of converting the natives. In this report he condemned conquest by force and urged that his system be put into practice. None of the colonists and few of the priests agreed with him, and there finally came a showdown.

In the mountains behind Guatemala was a territory called Tuzulutlan, inhabited by a savage tribe of Indians who had resisted conquest. The Spaniards had made several attempts to subdue them but had been so unsuccessful that they named this region *Tierra de Guerra,* Land of War. The colonists now dared Las Casas to attempt conquest of this section with the Cross alone.

Las Casas accepted the challenge on condition that no Spaniard be allowed to enter the territory for at least five years and that no Indians be taken in *encomienda* or forced to pay tribute. Despite great danger and hardships, the Dominican priests sent by Las Casas were able to penetrate this region and to put his principles into practice. In a short time they won over the caciques and eventually the rest of the natives. This admirable accomplishment of conversion through the Cross brought a new name for the land, *Vera Paz,* True Peace, and its capital was established.[4] But Las Casas did not remain long enough to make his experiment permanent. After he left Guatemala, the Spaniards broke the agreement, invaded the territory to exact tributes from the Indians and take many of them into slavery, and precipitated a large-scale revolt.

[3] *Op. cit.,* II, 348.
[4] *Ibid.,* 350.

Las Casas continued to press for social reform, and he gained some of his objectives because the power of the Church was growing steadily. The Council of the Indies, with its full authority over the New World, felt the influence of the Dominicans and of Las Casas. When Alonso de Maldonado, the president of the first *Audiencia* of Guatemala, attempted a reconciliation with Las Casas following a serious quarrel, the priest brushed him aside, exclaiming, "Away with you. You are excommunicated!"[5] Within a short time, Maldonado was replaced by Alonso López Cerrato, a monkish official whose severity in enforcing the laws was soon to bring protests from Bernal Díaz and many of the settlers.

Bernal left a record of how he felt about Las Casas and the Dominicans, but we may never know what he said about the man or the order. The twenty-two pages he wrote on the subject strangely disappeared from the Guatemalan archives more than a century ago.[6] The last two persons who reported seeing them were priests themselves, one of them a Dominican.

By the time Bernal Díaz was living in Guatemala, Las Casas had been successful in the promulgation of the New Laws of

---

[5] *Ibid.,* 307.

[6] In the Guatemalan archives, Brasseur de Bourbourg, a French historian-priest, found twenty-two pages in what was either a letter or a chapter written by Bernal Díaz and entitled "En contra de los religiosos de Santo Domingo." The manuscript was dated November 22, 1547. In his *Bibliothéque Mexique-Guatemalienne* (Paris, 1871), Bourbourg mentions this item as a copy made by one Fray Ximénez. The latter was a Dominican, while Bourbourg was a secular priest. The manuscript is not to be found in the Guatemalan archives, and a search in the libraries of the University of California and the Newberry Library, which received part of the materials collected by Bourbourg, has proved fruitless. Nor has it been uncovered in Paris or Vienna, where other Bourbourg materials were deposited. The manuscript may well have been destroyed.

1542, which were intended to give freedom to all natives held in bondage. But passage of laws and their observance were two different things. The colonists began to attack openly and to resist any attempt to have such laws enforced. Letters and petitions of protest were sent to Spain, and finally Bernal Díaz was chosen to lobby in the Spanish court on behalf of the Guatemala colonists.

Because of the role Bernal assumed in this conflict and because of the important effect the legislation was to have on future colonial life, it might be well to summarize what was happening. In many respects it was similar to our problem of slavery in the southern United States.

Indians held in *encomienda* had certain freedom as long as they worked the land held by the *encomendero* and paid him in tribute, or taxes, the amount fixed by law for each *encomienda*. Bernal Díaz could expect from his *encomiendas* an annual tribute of wheat, corn, fowl, eggs, and produce sufficient for him and his family to live on, with a surplus to be used for trading and bartering or to be turned into cash. The Indians on these lands were not considered slaves; they could not be sold nor in any way removed from their land. But during the Conquest and shortly after it, Bernal Díaz, as well as many of the conquerors and colonists, had obtained Indian prisoners as slaves. These Indians were the property of their captors, who could do with them as they chose. Each slave had a definite monetary value, and some colonists considered their wealth in the number of slaves they possessed.

Slavery, forced labor, and cruelty were nothing new to the Indians and were not introduced by the Spaniards, as Diego Rivera and other Mexican revolutionary figures of the *indigenista* school would have us believe. Slavery was practiced by the Aztecs, the Mayas, the Tlascalans, and others long before the Spaniards arrived. Montezuma and the lesser rulers imposed heavy tributes upon their subjects and meted out punishment to those who failed to comply. The great temples the Aztecs and the Mayan cultures left behind rose from the toil of forced labor.

The transition period which followed the Conquest was accomplished fairly easily because there was no real change in the condition of the Indians. They were long accustomed to similar demands made before the Conquest. There was little difference between working the soil for their Spanish masters and for their former caciques. There was not much of a change, either, from the construction of temples and pyramids to that of public buildings, churches, and convents. The trouble came, in most cases, not so much from cruelty (although there was plenty of that) as from the fact that the Spaniards did not know how to handle the natives. Indians acclimatized to the highlands were sent to work in the tropical lowlands; Indians from the lowlands were marched up into the highlands. In their greed, the Spaniards overworked the natives, and with the introduction of new diseases, to which the Indians had no immunity, thousands died. In many regions the death toll was appalling.

It is difficult to determine accurately the extent and degree of cruelty to the Indians in Guatemala, where Bernal Díaz had his *encomiendas,* but Bancroft believed that "nowhere was oppression carried to such an extreme as in Guatemala." Then he added that even the faithful Tlascaltecs, who had settled in Guatemala after the Conquest, were "enslaved, overworked and otherwise maltreated, until in 1547 there were barely a hundred survivors. The natives of Atitlán, who had never swerved in their allegiance to the Spaniards, were treated with equal severity. . . . If such was the treatment to which the most faithful allies of the Spaniards were subjected, what fell cruelties may we not expect to find inflicted on those who undeterred by defeat, rose again and again upon their oppressors? No word can depict the miseries of these hapless races. Wholesale slaughter, hanging, and burning, torturing, mutilating and branding followed the suppression of a revolt."[7]

But the natives of Guatemala were not docile lambs, either. They fought hard in battle and revolted at every opportunity. With the Spaniards they captured, they could be as cruel as had been the Aztecs.

Conditions, however, were serious enough, and the pleas of Las Casas before the royal council brought action in the form of the New Laws of 1542. These well-meaning laws were not fully enforced and the colonists protested so strongly that for a time they were even revoked. Nevertheless, the colonists were well aware that a change was bound to come. In their opinion, Las Casas was the man chiefly responsible for all their troubles and for having too vivid an imagination in describing back home the plight of the Indians.

At a meeting of the Guatemala *cabildo* attended by Bernal Díaz, a letter to the king was drafted which described in realistic terms how the colonists sized up Las Casas. Dated September 10, 1543, it reads in part:

> We have been assured that the instigator of this cruel sentence [the New Laws of 1542] is a certain Fray Bartolomé de las Casas. We are astonished, Unconquered Prince, that a matter initiated so long ago by your Catholic grandparents, passed through so many hands . . . should all come to naught through an unlettered, unholy, envious, vainglorious, hateful, and factious friar, not free from suspicion (for all of which abundant evidence can be sup-

[7] *Op. cit.,* II, 234.

plied), and above all else fond of stirring up trouble. So true is this last that he has not been in a single place in all these Indies from which he has not been expelled, nor is there a monastery that can put up with him. . . . In truth, Fray Bartolomé is the only good man and all the rest of us must be wicked.[8]

Native slaves in the colonies had by this time, as Simpson has stressed, "become an important article of commerce and many Spaniards had invested in them. Conceding their number to have been somewhere about two hundred thousand and their average value about twenty gold pesos apiece, we reach a very respectable figure, especially when we consider the scanty white population and the restricted areas in which slaves were used."[9]

The Guatemala *cabildo* again appealed to the king on August 31, 1544, but from a more practical viewpoint. In a long letter it summarized the colonists' stand with these words:

> Thus all the slaves would be set free and great inconveniences would arise. Not only would Your Majesty lose the revenue from the gold mined by the slaves, but the persons who own them would lose their property (as there are those who have no other property than the slaves they have purchased) and the land would suffer poverty and decrease, because there would be no gold mined or discovered. . . .[10]

At about this same period, Hernán Méndez, a *regidor* of the *cabildo* with whom Bernal Díaz served, presented a petition calling for a mass meeting to be held in the church to discuss the

[8] Quoted in Simpson, *Studies in the Administration of the Indians in New Spain,* IV, 9.

[9] *Ibid.,* 4–5.

[10] *Ibid.*

matter of the New Laws. Shortly afterward, Méndez was authorized to leave for Spain and to act as *procurador* on behalf of the colony.

The *cabildo* was not satisfied with the progress their cause was making, however, and before long the colonists contemplated sending another representative to lobby in their interests. For this job they later chose Bernal Díaz, but for the moment nothing further was done, the *cabildo* believing that the temporary revocation of the New Laws, which had just occurred, was all that was needed. But Las Casas was not asleep, and the *cabildo* soon discovered its mistake.

Early in 1548, while Bernal Díaz was a member of the *cabildo* and was holding the position of *procurador síndico,* or official solicitor, there came two important pieces of news. First was word of the death, in December of the previous year, of Bernal's long-time commander, Hernán Cortés. The passing of Cortés was profoundly felt by Bernal and the other conquerors in Guatemala who had served under him; it brought back to each recollections of that great adventure which was already becoming history.

The second piece of news was of a more serious nature, for it concerned the economic future of most of the settlers. This was the passage of a law which definitely established freedom of the slaves. The intentions of this legislation were quite clear in meaning, and from all indications, it would be strictly enforced. It read in part:

> We also command that no person, in war or in peace, may take, apprehend, use, sell or exchange as a slave, an Indian, or hold him as such, either by title of having got him in just war, or by purchase, trade, or exchange, or in any other way, or for any reason . . . on

pain that, if anyone should be found to have captured or to hold any Indian as slave, he shall incur the loss of all his goods . . . and the Indian . . . shall be immediately returned and restored to his own native land, in entire and natural liberty, at the cost of him who shall have captured him or held him as a slave. . . .[11]

When this royal measure was announced, the colonists were up in arms. It meant the end of retaining Indians in bondage, and it immediately affected Bernal Díaz, for he had early obtained a number of war prisoners as servants. Like most of the colonists, he felt they had come into his possession rightfully and that they should not now be taken from him. In the streets of Santiago, in the portals by the plaza, the veteran conquerors gathered to discuss the new legislation and ways to prevent its enforcement.

In the past, Bernal Díaz and the others might have depended on Maldonado, as the president of the *Audiencia,* to take their side in the struggle; but the good Maldonado was gone, and in his place was Alonso López Cerrato, one of those taciturn officials who had little sympathy for the colonists and who was as astute as he was zealous. While they could expect nothing from him, the *cabildo,* unable to turn to anyone else for the moment, nevertheless filed a protest with Cerrato, which would give them an extension of time. Bernal Díaz, as the official solicitor for the *cabildo,* probably helped to draft this letter:

The city has learned of your Lordship's commission concerning the slaves. . . . We have also heard that your Lordship has not been well informed in the matter and we are convinced that in a project of such moment and difficulty you will wish to consider, weigh and think over the consequences. And, if you do so, you will abandon the project, because your Lordship will discover that the whole well-being of these parts lies in the contentment and

[11] *Ibid.* 3.

permanent establishment of the Spaniards and in the small amount of silver and gold that is being mined, and not in the opinion of the religious.

. . . And you know, your Lordship, that the discharge of His Majesty's conscience, and yours in his name, and the good government of these parts, do not consist in freeing the Indians who are called slaves. . . . At present it is better for them to remain in our company than out of it, because we consider most of them as though they were our own children. And, if in times past there was some carelessness in their treatment, it is no longer true . . . rather, they are beholden to us for having reared them. . . .[12]

This appeal, as expected, fell on deaf ears. Cerrato knew all the arguments and all the answers; besides, he owed his appointment as president of the *Audiencia* to Las Casas, and the latter had not put him there without a purpose. Cerrato did not, as far as the records show, reply to this letter.

The *cabildo,* now using either municipal funds or contributions collected from each settler, decided, in a last desperate attempt, to take its case before the Council of the Indies—and, if necessary, before the king. For this project, Bernal Díaz was chosen. The *cabildo* of Guatemala, however, was not alone in its plans to lobby before the royal council. Mexico and Peru were also working toward the same objective and had assigned *procuradores* to represent them in Spain.

We do not have the exact date Bernal left for the mother country. Simpson believes it was in 1549, although Bernal, not always accurate on dates, says he went to Spain in 1550. At least he was in Castile that year and most of 1551, but in his writings he was rather cagey about the real purpose of his trip and does not mention that he was authorized by the *cabildo* to go there.

[12] *Ibid.,* 6–7.

He suggests that the call came from Spain. "They sent for me because I was the oldest conqueror in New Spain," he blithely observes.

No one summoned him. He went there on orders of the *cabildo* and as its official solicitor he represented the town council and the colonists. He says he was in Spain chiefly in the interests of establishing the perpetuity of *encomiendas,* which he was. Another main objective of his appearance before the royal council was to plead against the emancipation of the slaves. We have it in his own words in a letter which recently turned up in Guatemala bearing the date of February 1, 1549. This is a long and tedious appeal addressed to the Council of the Indies:

> Very Powerful Sirs:
> Bernal Díaz, *procurador síndico* of this city of Santiago of Guatemala, has the honor of addressing your Highnesses on behalf of the said city and for those whom I represent and to advise you that your president and *oidores* of the Royal *Audiencia* in this city have under certain penalties of the law ordered all those who have Indian slaves to bring them forth so they may be set free. Furthermore, they have publicly proclaimed this order by the town crier in the plaza and even before this action was taken they have already given freedom to some slaves, by which action they have caused great harm to all of the republic and provinces. Because of these harmful effects which have taken place and speaking with proper respect in the name of the said order and in view of previous pleas, I beg anew before your Highnesses to reconsider these actions and to request your president and *oidores* in your kingdom of Spain to do the same for the following reasons:
> The first because the Indians were made slaves in accordance with royal provisions and conforming to the instructions of the Royal *Audiencia* which is proven by the certificate given to Pedro de Alvarado our governor at the time. . . .
> The second reason because those who were made slaves were

128

already slaves of the Indian caciques who owned them and were not made slaves by your governors. While they were branded, this was only done so that these slaves could be used by the Spaniards who bought them and to avoid that others might take possession of them.

The third reason, because the caciques and others who owned them sold these slaves publicly in the market place and during this period our governors and Spaniards merely requested official license to buy them, which was granted by royal order. . . .

The fourth reason, because the slaves bought by the Spaniards are better treated by the Christians than by the Indians who sacrificed them to their idols and in these sacrifices many died. . . .

Another reason, because those won in wars were justifiably taken and by royal license and in accordance with your instructions . . . because at the time our Empress and our lady of glorious memory ordered that no more slaves should be taken, this order was obeyed and no more slaves were made, although no mention was made of what had been done in the past or that it was wrongly done. . . .

Still one more reason: that because the new law given by His Majesty to these parts, which refers specifically to slaves, does not order the *Audiencia* publicly to proclaim the law, nor does it give freedom to all the slaves, but merely gives the right of each slave to ask for freedom, etc. . . . etc. . . .

. . . I humbly plead that in the name of the colonists and in my name justice be granted.[13]

Bernal Díaz

Bernal and his companions were quibbling. Their arguments had certain justification and the colony did suffer economic hardships as a consequence of the new law, but no real reason why the legislation should be revoked was given. Even if such a reason had existed, it would have been of no use: Las Casas

[13] *Ibid.*, 32–36.

was present to tear down every argument raised. Besides, the royal council and Prince Philip, already being groomed to be the next king, had made up their minds. The pleas of Bernal Díaz and others lobbying before the court were flatly denied. The law remained on the books and the council enforced it as strictly as possible. Slavery in name was at an end, but forced labor remained constant.

This law in no way changed the status of the Indians held in *encomienda*. They were generally accepted as free men who could do as they chose as long as they worked the land and paid taxes to their *encomenderos*. They could be neither sold nor transferred to other land. As a group they were oppressed, though abuses against individuals were the exception, not the rule. Not until the *encomienda* system broke down were they completely on their own.

The word *encomienda* comes from the verb *encomendar,* to entrust or to be committed to another's protection. This was the purpose of the *encomiendas,* and an *encomendero* had the Indians under his protection only for his lifetime and that of his heir. When Bernal Díaz and the others failed to revoke the law against slavery, they now turned their talents and their argu-ments toward the perpetuation of the *encomiendas.* This would mean that the Indians would remain forever with the family holding an *encomienda* and not revert to the crown upon the death of an *encomendero.*

The reasons Bernal Díaz and his colleagues gave for the per-petuation of the *encomiendas* were many. They argued that if perpetuity rights were granted, the landowners would show greater interest toward the native workers and would assist in converting them to the Holy Faith; that if the natives became ill, they would be treated by the *encomenderos* as if they were children and medicines would be provided for them; that the proprietors of the land would improve it by increasing the acreage of vines planted, as well as by raising better cattle; and above all, that the soldiers and colonists who had served His Majesty in the past would be tranquil in knowing that their own families would be taken care of in the event of their deaths and that their incomes would not be distributed to others.

Yet some of the reasons they enumerated were the very ones they had promised to uphold on being granted *encomiendas*. From the first their obligation was to convert the natives and to look after them. Las Casas, who was present at these discussions before the Council of the Indies, pointed this out at once and strongly protested any attempt to perpetuate the *encomienda* system. The council, after listening to both sides, postponed a decision and the whole question was tabled.

If Bernal Díaz failed in his mission to Spain, he at least appeared to have enjoyed himself thoroughly, for he had been in his element, giving advice to others and rubbing shoulders with the great and the near-great of the time. He had been not just a conqueror but the legal representative of one of the important Spanish colonies. He had tangled in arguments with Las Casas, with Vasco de Quiroga, the famed bishop of Michoacán, with Tomás de San Martín, bishop of Charcas, and he had met and talked with the powerful Marqués de Mondéjar, president of the Council of the Indies.

Yet for Bernal Díaz, always the opportunist, this was not enough. He next turned his attention to his own needs and interests. This time, he hoped, he would not return from Spain as empty handed as on his previous trip.

11 𝄞 "*FAVOR HIM WITH WHAT HE NEEDS*"

IN Santiago de Guatemala, Teresa, the wife of Bernal Díaz, and their two children, Francisco and Pedro, waited for his return from Spain. The months stretched into a year and then another year approached. If he wrote to his family of what he was doing, of his hopes and his plans, no one bothered to save such letters. Even the official records of the *cabildo* for this period, which would carry some news about their representative in Spain, have disappeared.

Yet Bernal Díaz was not wasting his time. He was making full use of every opportunity to further himself, as we know from documents on file in the archives of Seville. During his various appearances before the Council of the Indies on behalf of the Guatemala colonists, he had become acquainted with the members of the council. From them he now sought what help he could get for himself and his family. He realized that he might never have a similar chance, and he made the most of it.

As usual, he pleaded poverty and lack of recognition. He complained that he had been badly treated and maneuvered out of the land he had possessed in Mexico. He was not asking for riches but for what he justifiably deserved as one of the oldest conquerors and settlers, he told them. He had a wife and growing children to support, to educate, and to marry; the land and Indians he had were not enough to provide for his family in his old age. He would even welcome, he informed them, an official post with a modest salary in which his experience and knowledge of years of dealing with the natives would be of value. There was a daughter who had to be married off and another daughter in Mexico who was ill and needed help. He, Bernal Díaz, who should be wealthy, was poor because he had always acted unselfishly and only in the interests of the king. He would always continue to do so, and he was therefore placing his case at the mercy of the royal council. He asked their consideration of his claims.

Bernal had a warm personality and he was a good talker. He could plead poverty better than any other conqueror. The members of the council listened and eventually acted. The first gesture benefiting him was a *cédula* dated December 1, 1550. Given in the name of the king and queen, it reads in part:

> . . . And now on behalf of Bernal Díaz, resident of the city of Santiago de Guatemala, he has related to me that he asked *Licenciado* Maldonado, at that time governor of the said province, that conforming with our letter [this refers to a *cédula* granted in 1540] he would receive compensation for the towns of Indians which were taken away from him and that in accordance with our instructions, this was carried out. . . .
>
> But the Indians granted to him brought him little profit and he was promised others when they became available . . . but this was not done. . . . When you, *Licenciado* Cerrato, succeeded to the presidency of the *Audiencia,* he made a similar appeal to you, but you refused him. . . . If the said Bernal Díaz has not received lands and

Indians of equal value as those previously held, I order you to give him those that first become available . . . and while waiting for this compensation, the said Bernal Díaz should be given in the province of Guatemala an appropriate official post. . . .[1]

I the Queen, By Order of Her Majesty

The use of the names of the king and queen was a formality which the Council of the Indies employed in all transactions and in all documents. There is no indication that Bernal was ever received by either the king or the queen; both, as a matter of fact, were in Germany nearly all of the time Bernal was in Spain.

Two grown daughters of Bernal, both born out of wedlock, now enter rather obliquely into the picture. The first, Teresa Díaz de Padilla, was married and a resident in Coatzacoalcos, while the second and younger one was apparently living in Guatemala. This latter daughter Bernal was anxious to marry off well, and if he did not plan to provide her with a dowry, he at least intended to get a government post for her future husband. On January 24, 1551, he obtained for her the following *cédula:*

I the King. To the President and *oidores* of our Royal *Audiencia* of the Confines: Bernal Díaz . . . has related to me that he is one of the first discoverers and conquerors of New Spain and that at present he is married and residing in the said city with his wife and children, and among whom is one a young woman of marriageable age. He has therefore asked me to order you to provide the person whom she marries with a position befitting his category. . . . Having the wish to favor her, I hereby order that the person she marries be helped and aided and that he be given a position in our service. . . .[2]

I the Queen

[1] Cabañas, III, 308–309.
[2] Cédula of January 24, 1551, in Paso y Troncoso, *op. cit.,* VI, 28.

The elder daughter, Teresa Díaz de Padilla, appeared on the scene two months later when on March 21, 1551, Bernal obtained a *cédula* on her behalf. From this document we know she held an *encomienda* in Coatzacoalcos, that she was ill and sought permission to have her *encomienda* rights transferred to either Guatemala or some other region with a more healthful climate; failing in this plea she asked that she be given permission to abandon her *encomienda* while she underwent medical treatment. The *cédula* is addressed to the president of the *Audiencia* and reads in part:

> I the King. To *Licenciado* Cerrato, etc., etc. On behalf of Teresa Díaz de Padilla, daughter of Bernal Díaz, resident of the city of Guatemala, who has related to us that she has a town of Indians in *encomienda* ... that she wishes to leave it and place it in the hands of the Crown, in lieu of which she asks that she be granted an equivalent *encomienda* in the province of Guatemala or Mexico. She asks this because she is very sick and cannot recover from her illnesses in the said province and furthermore, she fears that if she remains there, she will die. And if the aforementioned cannot be carried out, she implores us to give her permission to absent herself from her *encomienda* while she undergoes treatment in Mexico or in the province of Guatemala without the penalty of losing her land. . . . I order that she be given the permission she asks.[3]
>
> *I the Queen. By order of Her Majesty*

This is the last we hear of Teresa Díaz de Padilla. She does not appear mentioned by name in any other record nor is she ever referred to again. The same is true of the daughter who had been living in Bernal's household in Guatemala and for whom he had requested a position for her prospective husband. Much guessing

---

[3] Cédula of March 21, 1551, *ibid.*, 35–36.

can be done about these daughters and what became of them, but there is no evidence to support any conjecture. Their mother was a native woman, and Bernal lived with her for a time. Some of the conquerors did marry their native women, but if Bernal had done so, in the eyes of the Church he could not have wed Teresa Becerra as he did, unless, of course, his first wife had died.

The fact that he brought a daughter by another woman into his house was not unusual in those days. Pedro de Alvarado's illegitimate daughter, Doña Leonor, lived in his household, was a companion to his wife, and later even married his wife's cousin, Francisco de la Cueva. If church records for this period were still available, we would be able to establish who finally married Bernal's younger daughter and perhaps also obtain her mother's name. But lacking such information, we are forced to leave her and her sister and turn again to the activities of their father in Castile.

Bernal planned at this time to take back with him certain articles he purchased in Spain for his use and as gifts for his wife and children, for he requested and was granted a *cédula* giving him the right to bring into Guatemala free of duty such merchandise as would not exceed five hundred pesos in value.[4]

Also for the same date, January 24, 1551, we come across another document which is curious enough in its contents, as well as in showing the tight hold the crown had on the colonists. To import into Guatemala free of duty three jackasses, Bernal had to get permission from the Council of the Indies as follows:

> I the King. For the present I give license and authority to you, Bernal Díaz, resident of the city of Santiago de Guatemala, so that from this kingdom you may take with you to the said province of Guatemala, free of duty, three stallion asses which do not belong

[4] Cédula of January 24, 1551, *ibid.*, 29–30.

to the Indies, and because you will use them for breeding purposes, I extend this favor and I order it be done without any further impediment. . . .[5]

I the Queen

Four days later, on January 28, Bernal managed to get still another *cédula* directed to *Licenciado* Cerrato, president of the *Audiencia* in Guatemala.[6] In this one, Bernal's services to his king are again recounted and it is stressed that during the period he lived in the provinces of Coatzacoalcos and Tabasco he carried out efficiently the duties of *visitador,* or official inspector, and saw to it that the Indians working in *encomiendas* were well treated.

The royal instructions then go on to state that because the said Bernal Díaz has considerable knowledge and experience in dealing with the natives, *Licenciado* Cerrato is ordered to appoint him *visitador* for one of the most important provinces under the jurisdiction of the *Audiencia.* The *cédula* concludes with directions "that you aid and favor him with what he needs and give him charge of such things in which he can best serve us."

Under the same date Bernal was given a second *cédula* which is important in its contents, for it indicates that Bernal feared he had made certain enemies whose animosity toward him was such that they threatened his life.[7] Who these possible enemies were or why they were after Bernal is something of a mystery. But the facts are that Bernal asked and was granted the rights to have armed bodyguards.

How can it be that this veteran soldier, who had faced death so many times, whose body was covered with scars of wounds,

[5] *Ibid.*
[6] Cabañas, III, 341.
[7] *Ibid.,* 342.

should suddenly ask for protection? Why should he who had been in such tight spots before now fear he might be killed in the open streets of the city where he lived and where he held public office? Did the brave and valiant Bernal Díaz become a coward overnight? He has told us that before a battle his heart was in his throat, that he trembled and was often afraid, but this is not unusual, even among the bravest of soldiers. "We feared death, because we were men," Bernal relates on another occasion, and that is not the statement of a coward.

What, then, frightened him? The historian Valle-Arizpe says that Bernal became involved in serious arguments, though he does not suggest what they might be, and that "certain individuals full of hatred were set to kill him." He adds that "the years took away his courage. He had little strength left and he was weakened and without force. The years and old age finish with everything."[8] A rather unlikely story, for Bernal was then fifty-four and had thirty more years of good living ahead. José Millá y Vidaurre, a Guatemalan historian of the last century, advanced a more logical reason. He pointed out that there continued to come to Guatemala from Spain persons with royal charters waiting for *encomiendas* to become vacant. "These created a troublesome situation among the old conquerors and first settlers," he wrote, "because they felt these persons sought their death in order to take over their *encomiendas*."[9]

Yet duels and violent deaths by murder were not common in either Guatemala or Mexico in the post-Conquest period. Strict discipline was maintained throughout the colonies, and there was always the gallows in the public square for those who disobeyed the primary laws. Few went armed, and the fact that

[8] *Op. cit.*, 309.
[9] *Historia de la América central*, I, 163.

Bernal had to get a royal permit for him and his servants to carry weapons is another indication of how rigidly the colonists were governed. It had to be that way, for many of these men were hardened and reckless, and their Latin temperaments not only brought angry words but often started feuds.

In character, Bernal Díaz was not much different from the others. He was certainly not such a lovable old soldier as some historians have painted him; he was sensuous, sharp tempered, jealous, and proud, as he had a right to be, of his accomplishments. He was sometimes egotistical to the point of being crude, and he was sensitive to the slightest criticism; with his constant advice, he was bound to make enemies. At least the *cédula* granted to him bears this out. It reads in part:

I the King. To the President and *oidores* of our Royal *Audiencia* of the Confines: Bernal Díaz . . . has related to me that he has certain enemies in that land, for which reason he has the need to be guarded by two servants with offensive and defensive weapons, and because of them, he has requested me to favor him with a license so that he and his two servants may bear arms . . . and when the said Bernal Díaz after having given bond and having paid the necessary fee and after complying with the terms of this *cédula* so that he and his two servants will not affront anyone with the said weapons which are to be used solely for defensive purposes . . . give him license for six years . . . his servants may carry such arms only when traveling and throughout the Indies, islands and the continent of the Ocean Sea . . . and having given him a license, we order that in whatever city, town or village, he may be in, he and his two servants may be permitted to bear arms, even though their possession is prohibited. . . .[10]

I the Queen

[10] Cabañas, III, 342.

The historian Cabañas, in his introduction to the Mexican edition of Bernal Díaz' work, stresses this *cédula* as further evidence that Bernal was not as poor as he described himself to be, for if he were in such poverty, the permit would not cover all of the "Indies, islands and the continent of the Ocean Sea," and he could not afford the expenses of the two bodyguards, nor risk having enemies. But that wording was standard terminology in *cédulas* of this type, and the fact that Bernal Díaz had two servants to protect him does not indicate in any way that he was rich. Servants were paid very little and even to this day some of the poorer families in Mexico and Guatemala have domestic help. Bernal was not poverty stricken, but there is no evidence that he was rich, either. If he was, he certainly would not have been so anxious to obtain a government post, with its modest compensation.

As late as June 13, 1551, shortly before his departure from Spain, Bernal again appeared before the Council of the Indies and petitioned for still another *cédula* which might get him an "official position with a competent salary." This *cédula* mentions that he should be entitled to additional consideration because he is "related to those who have been our servants." Bernal must have reminded the council of his father's services as *regidor* of Medina del Campo.

When Bernal Díaz sailed from the port of Sanlúcar de Barrameda in the summer of that year, his future appeared a great deal brighter than on his last trip. He was firmly established in Guatemala, he was a member of the *cabildo,* he had a wife of some social position, he held *encomiendas,* and in his leather case were documents which should materially improve his prospects and those of his family. He had failed in his original mission to Spain, but this had not been his fault; the pleas from the others had also been denied. He had, however, gained considerable experience and knowledge and had made many new friends. He would have plenty to tell his companions in Guatemala. Bernal had enjoyed his extended stay in Spain, but he was glad he was going home. This was his last trip to the Old World.

It would be illuminating to learn what Bernal took with him from Spain in the wooden chests which accompanied him on the return voyage. There must have been gifts of brocade and silk for his wife, material for himself, and something for his grown daughter and for his two boys, Francisco and Pedro.

Shortly after his arrival in the city of Santiago, on September 1 of the same year, he presented himself before *Licenciado* Alonso López Cerrato, president of the *Audiencia,* and Diego de Robledo, royal notary. According to a document on file in the archives, Bernal produced on this occasion only the *cédula* dealing with a request for an official position in the government.[11] Cerrato, as president of the *Audiencia,* took the *cédula* and, as was the custom, "kissed it and placed it over his head and said he would obey and comply with all His Majesty ordered." The witnesses at this proceeding were Gonzalo Hidalgo and Alonso de Aguilar.

Licenciado Cerrato may have been responsible for Bernal's appointment, for life, as *regidor* of the *cabildo* of Guatemala, a position he was to hold until his death. If Cerrato was responsible, Bernal, in his next appearance before the *Audiencia,* found him in quite another frame of mind. Bernal wrote that every time a conqueror came before him, Cerrato assumed an attitude unbecoming a high official of the king. His face, according to Bernal, would take on a fierce look and, shaking from emotion, he would cry out: "Who sent you to conquer this land? Did His

11 *Ibid.,* 309–10.

Majesty send you? Then show me his orders! Is it not enough what you have already stolen?"[12]

Bernal had not obtained easily his *cédulas* from the Council of the Indies. He had pulled strings, he had cornered members of the council, and he had addressed them in a body. He had worked hard those many months in Spain, and he was not going to let this taciturn and aloof Cerrato undo everything he had done. The council, in the name of the king, had given their instructions; they were meant to be carried out and not disregarded.

Bernal, however, as well as the other conquerors and colonists, soon discovered that Cerrato was firm and stubborn and retained his icy manner, never warming up to their demands. Even the *cabildo,* the official body of the municipality, was at odds with the president of the *Audiencia.*

Historians are not entirely in accord with the views of the *cabildo* and of Bernal Díaz about Cerrato. Millá called Cerrato one of the best—if not the best—presidents of that period, adding that "he was known as the father and protector of the natives."[13] Bancroft appears to be in agreement, pointing out that while Cerrato played hand in hand with the priests, he did much to alleviate the suffering of the natives. He quotes one Guatemala settler as saying about Cerrato: "Our day has passed and that of the friars has begun."[14]

The colonists hated Cerrato and strove to oust him from office. At last Bernal took matters into his own hands. On February 22, 1552, he picked up pen and paper and this time he addressed himself to the highest authority, the king.

[12] *Ibid.,* 349.
[13] *Op. cit.,* I, 110.
[14] *Op. cit.,* II, 309.

Bernal was in a temper, and a study of the long letter shows signs of confused thinking. This document lacks the simple style which marks his later literary work. He must have suffered some misgivings in attacking the governor of the province; he obviously feared retribution if the letter should fall into Cerrato's hands. In part, this is what he wrote:

Sacred Imperial Catholic Majesty:

As I am known to your Royal Council of the Indies and as I have served Your Majesty from youth to old age with great loyalty and fidelity and because I am your *regidor* in this city of Guatemala, and for many other reasons, I dare to make known what is being done in the governing of these lands, and further because it is believed by Your Majesty and the Royal Council of the Indies that all which is ordered is complied with; these orders sent all being very just and for the welfare of the Indians as well as the Spaniards and good for the land. I kiss the sacred feet of Your Majesty. . . .

Know Your Majesty that as I have said, there is a necessity for justice at this time, because before everything moved along much better, that is for the Indians and their perpetuation; and seeing this I dare to relate what I know so that this situation will not worsen. And since a year ago I was in the royal court and at the time I left there, there came to these provinces the *Licenciado* Cerrato as president and at once he gave indications of wishing to do justice. . . . That is why I did not complain about him when I was in the royal court, but if I did not advise you now, I would feel guilty.

But know, Your Majesty, that everything he does is contrary to your royal orders. . . . He has spoken sometimes of governors who robbed, cheated and did ugly things and that he is not of the type to receive presents, not even a chicken, nor has he dallied with any neighbor's wife. . . . Yet he fails to see that a *repartimiento* of land he has given to a relative is worth more than a chicken . . . and in truth, as I was a few months ago in the royal court and saw your presidents and *oidores* and saw how correct and what good justice they grant and how agreeable they are in giving their answers . . . and when I see what is happening here . . . .

Oh, Sacred Majesty, how just and good are the royal orders you send to these provinces and how they falsify them here and do what they wish with them! And this I say because I see the friars with ambition to domineer and rule these lands, and Cerrato with greediness to enrich himself and his relatives . . . these friars know and understand his nature and they will not let Your Majesty hear the truth. . . .

I implore Your Majesty to please order that this letter does not fall into the hands of Cerrato, because others which have been written by the *cabildo* on matters of your royal service have been returned. . . .

I kiss the sacred feet of Your Imperial Catholic Majesty.[15]

Bernal Díaz

There was no reply to this letter from the king. The following year, either through pressure or ill health, Cerrato resigned from the presidency of the *Audiencia*.

[15] Cabañas, II, 345–52.

12 ✣ SO THAT THE WORLD WILL KNOW

THE resignation of Cerrato was greeted triumphantly by the conquerors and colonists of Guatemala, and by Bernal Díaz it was accepted as a personal victory. Had he not written to the king? Had not His Majesty read his letter and acted accordingly? Over good Malaga wine in his home and in those of his friends, Bernal discussed this welcome piece of news and boasted of his part in bringing it about. Now if the *cabildo* would only listen to some further advice he had to give, they would all be the better for it . . . .

Bernal's letter was neither instrumental in nor did it have anything to do with forcing Cerrato from power.[1] But the writing of this letter does suggest that it brought the necessary stimulus which Bernal needed to begin his famous history.

There is reason to believe that as early as 1540, when he was in Spain, Bernal Díaz turned over in his mind the possibility of writing a sort of memoir of his experiences in which he could

---

[1] On Cerrato's fall, see Millá y Vidaurre, *op. cit.,* I, 110ff.

defend the conquerors as well as call attention to himself. His move to Guatemala and other events shaping his career interrupted such plans as he may have had for preparing this work, but the idea was never lost and in fact cropped up from time to time for further consideration.

It was not easy for a man of Bernal's character, one who was no scholar and who had previously written very little, to sit down and tackle a major literary effort. He must have questioned his ability and his knowledge. It was difficult for him to write, and he found that to form phrases with an appealing sound required patience and a skill which he felt he did not possess. The very letter he wrote to the king, in its original Spanish, shows how forced the words were and what a hard time he had in conveying his thoughts. When he finished it, he probably submitted it to friends for criticism and corrections and then to an *escribano* for copying. Finally it was sent, and lo and behold it had brought about the desired results!

Now if he could do the same in describing the conquest of New Spain and the part he and the other soldiers had taken in it—if he were capable of doing that, he could support the rights of the conquerors and the colonists and adroitly touch upon his own accomplishments. Besides, it would serve as an affidavit of what he had done, seen, and heard and would be a record he could leave behind for his children.

He had at this time only a vague idea of what he was going to put to paper and how it might take shape. His commander, Cortés, had already told the story in published letters, but it was all from a personal viewpoint.

He, Bernal Díaz, would do it by enlarging the scope of operations, by taking the side of the soldiers, and by making sure credit went to those who deserved it, like himself and others who had seldom been mentioned by Cortés.

Bernal began his *True History* as a personal narrative, as an eyewitness account of what he saw, what he did, and what he remembered. Like all writers, he probably had a difficult time getting started; and he wrote slowly, laboring over phrases, trying to portray with sincerity the great drama in which he had played an important role.

Bernal was convinced that he had a story to tell, so that "the world will know" what manner of men were the conquerors and what they had achieved for their king. But the problem of writing must have appeared to him insurmountable. Yes, he had written letters to the king, but writing a long book was something else. He lacked the necessary confidence, and he felt he did not have the scholarly refinements required for the elaboration of the work he dreamed about.

Nevertheless, the ambition to write an account of the Conquest from the soldier's point of view overcame all the obstacles which Bernal knew he faced. He was stubborn and persistent, and once he had made up his mind, nothing could dissuade him.

We do not know how much time he spent writing the opening chapters of his book. Sometimes weeks and many months passed when he did not write a single line. Bernal led an active life taking care of his properties, and his duties as *regidor* occupied a considerable part of his routine.

During this period there were many happenings in the colony which disturbed Bernal and which resulted in his laying aside his manuscript. The successor to Cerrato had not turned out to be much of an improvement, and there was discontent among the Spaniards, including Bernal, who had always hoped for an *Audiencia* president more sympathetic to their interests.

Late in 1555, there came to Guatemala rumors of the contemplated abdication of Charles V as king and emperor. These reports were confirmed by an official notice of the abdication

147

which the *cabildo* of Guatemala received in January of the following year. The new monarch was the devout Prince Philip, named "King and Ruler of Spain, Flanders, and the Indies." But not until May of 1557 did the *cabildo* decide to raise the official standard in the name of King Philip II. This flag, according to the records of the *cabildo,* was made of damask in crimson and blue colors and bore the coats of arms of His Majesty and of the city.

Bernal Díaz was among those who signed the order that "as many persons and officials as possible shall accompany the flag which will be brought out from the building occupied by the *cabildo* and then taken to the palace of the Royal *Audiencia* . . . on the night of the day that this is done, all the citizens and residents shall participate and illuminate their houses."[2]

On July 26, the day selected for this ceremony, the *regidores* asked the secretary to read the royal notification concerning the new king, and this order was then kissed and placed above their heads. Then, in unison, Bernal and other city officials repeated that they would obey and be faithful and loyal to the king. The flag was now turned over to Francisco López, the *alcalde ordinario,* and the members of the *cabildo* went to the roof of the building where it was unfurled before the people. As they raised the standard, they cried out: "Guatemala, Guatemala for King Philip, our Lord and King of Castile, León and the Indies!"

The ceremony was followed by vespers and benediction at the cathedral, and on the next night there were *fiestas* and processions led by the principal residents of the city, who rode on horses and carried lighted torches. Bernal Díaz was among those who participated in this affair.

When Alvarado, Marín, and Bernal Díaz were in Guatemala

[2] Francisco de Paula García Peláez, *Memorias para la historia del antiguo reino de Guatemala,* II, *cap.* lxxix.

on their return from Honduras in 1528, a revolt had broken out among the natives and the Spaniards were forced to subdue them. The actual victory over the natives did not occur, however, until Santa Cecilia Day, November 22. From time to time the city of Santiago de Guatemala had commemorated this day with appropriate honor, and the official standard was usually carried by the oldest *regidor*. Bernal Díaz was not the oldest *regidor* in Guatemala in 1557; this distinction was shared by Francisco López and Francisco de la Cueva. But since those two had previously carried the flag during the *fiestas* for His Majesty, the *cabildo,* meeting on September 1, chose Bernal for the honor.[3]

Thus on the morning of November 22, Bernal, accompanied by the other city officials, led the procession from the building of the *cabildo* through the streets of the city and then to the cathedral, where religious services were held. Again there were *fiestas,* dances in the patios of the homes, fireworks, and on the following day bullfights and *juegos de caña,* jousting tournaments of knights on horseback armed with reeds instead of lances. Bernal, with his sense of the dramatic and his great desire for recognition and importance, must have thoroughly enjoyed himself.

The *fiestas* on these occasions were gay affairs with much time and money lavished upon them. The wives and daughters of the Spaniards donned their finest clothes, made of material imported from France and Spain at considerable cost; this usually consisted of a flowing skirt of either brocade or velvet, a sleeveless jacket laced with gold or silver cord, and a mantilla draped gracefully over their shoulders. A large comb imbedded with precious stones gave height to the women and set off their hair; earrings and other jewelry were often worth fortunes.

[3] *Ibid.*

The men wore blouses of velvet or silk with close-fitting sleeves open between the elbows and shoulders to show off their fine linen shirts; they used long stockings, snug underpants, and wide breeches which they called *gregüescos*. A scabbard containing a dagger completed the costume. Yet no Spaniard was fully dressed who did not have a rich cape which was thrown aside when he was indoors. So extravagant were the clothes of the wealthier colonists that on a number of occasions the king issued orders prohibiting the use of brocade and other expensive materials for such ostentatious display.[4]

On special days there were receptions in the palace of the *Audiencia,* although the festivities were generally restricted to the patios of private homes. These patios were decorated with masses of flowers and greens, and always there were long tables of food: wild game of many classes, including ducks, turkeys, doves, and quail; fish from the fresh water of the lake and from the sea; and whole roasted pigs and calves. Fruits were plentiful in this temperate altitude of Guatemala and among the favorites were sapotes, granadillas, melons, annonas, and the tuna, or red fruit of the cactus plant. Thomas Gage, the erstwhile Dominican, reports that the Spaniards esteemed the tuna fruit, "although it doth colour and dye the eater's mouth, lips and apparel, yea and maketh the urine look like pure blood." There was a variety of vegetables, such as tomatoes, avocados, chayotes (boiled or baked), squash, yucca roots, sweet potatoes, and all kinds of chilies for flavoring. Wine from Spain, and some by this time from Peru, flowed generously from casks or *botijas*.

At these *fiestas* and banquets there were servants for each guest, and the affairs frequently lasted until the early hours of

---

[4] See J. Joaquín Pardo, *Prontuario de reales cédulas, 1529–1599,* for numerous examples of sumptuary legislation.

the morning, only to continue the next day. Shops were closed, and no one bothered about work as long as the celebration went on. Preoccupations about the future and difficulties with the government were brushed aside as the Spaniards ate, drank, and danced.

The marimba, the national instrument of Guatemala, was unknown in those days.[5] Not until later was it introduced by the African slaves, who by using hollow native woods improvised an instrument that was quickly adopted as their own by the Indians. In the middle of the sixteenth century, the Spaniards depended on guitars, flutes, trumpets, and sackbuts, an early type of slide trombone, at their fiestas and official functions. As we learn from Bernal Díaz, there was a certain amount of drunkenness, which led to disputes. Often, however, the presence of a bishop or priests restrained the celebrants.

Aside from these *fiestas,* one of the developments which at this time greatly pleased the colonists of Guatemala was the admitted failure by the Dominican priests of their attempt to subdue the natives by spiritual guidance instead of the sword. In Vera Paz, where Bartolomé de las Casas had begun his experiment in peaceful conquest, many tribes were now in revolt. The most violent of these were the Lacandóns, who were undisciplined and savage, as remnants of the tribe are to this day.

Between 1555 and 1558 the depredations of the Lacandóns reached such proportions that Spaniards were killed in raids on several towns in Chiapas, and it began to look as if the entire territory of Vera Paz would have to be abandoned. In desperation the Dominicans asked the *Audiencia* to provide men and

[5] No chronicler of the sixteenth century ever mentions the marimba, which is nearly impossible if the instrument had been used. There is reason to believe that the instrument was of African origin, introduced later, and is not native to Guatemala, as is generally assumed.

arms to subdue the Indians, but the *Audiencia* rejected their request on the ground that it could not declare war against the natives. The appeal was finally carried to the king.

Early in 1559, the *Audiencia* of Guatemala received royal orders to organize an expedition against the Lacandóns at once. The decree was publicly proclaimed in the town square and volunteers were asked to join the ranks on the promise that all prisoners captured were to become lawful slaves—the antislavery legislation was for the moment officially forgotten. As a further inducement, generous grants of land were guaranteed.

The thrill of seeing men prepare for this adventure must have stirred old memories in the heart of the aging Bernal Díaz. But if he ever considered joining up, it was only a passing thought. He was approaching his middle sixties, and although he could still ride a horse as well as the younger men and still had a great deal of endurance, he was better at reminiscing about the days of the Conquest than at taking part in new exploits. It was well that Bernal stayed at home; the expedition was an expensive failure, for as soon as the Spaniards approached, the Lacandóns disappeared into the back country and the number of prisoners seized was small. The disappointed colonists returned to Guatemala cursing the royal order that had sent them on a hazardous and unprofitable chase.

While the expedition was having its troubles, so was Bernal. He learned that the Indians of his *encomiendas* at San Pedro and San Juan Zacatepec—four leagues from Guatemala—had secretly sold some of this land to a certain Spaniard named Francisco del Valle, who had already taken possession of it.

Bernal quickly protested to the *Audiencia,* claiming that the Indians had not realized what they were doing and now regretted the sale. He also charged that Del Valle, as *factor,* or public commissioner for the city, had used his official standing in influencing the Indians to part with the property. If the deal went through, Bernal knew, he would lose tributes paid to him by the Indians, though behind his protest was also an earnest effort to protect them from giving up land they needed. He was convinced that Del Valle had deceived the Indians.

Unable to get satisfaction from the *Audiencia* and fearing that Del Valle might get favorable action from the Council of the Indies, Bernal, on February 20, 1558, wrote to King Philip II:

Catholic and Royal Majesty:
I have learned that one Francisco del Valle, our *factor*, has sent your Royal Council of the Indies a request that they favor him with certain lands which he wishes to develop and which are located between the Indian towns of San Pedro and San Juan. . . . This *factor* purchased in company of one Balderrama certain lands from the caciques of these towns already mentioned by me and for which I am the *encomendero*, and this was done without my knowing anything about it and I was therefore unable to hinder the sale. . . . The Indians being ignorant of how much land is twelve *caballerías* and realizing they have been deceived, they now demand that the transaction be annulled.
Before your Royal *Audiencia* they have asked justice and are willing to return the pesos of gold which they received in payment . . . and this the caciques do because truly they are dissatisfied with him [Del Valle] and for the bad way he has treated them . . . and if it were not for me and the Dominican priests who reside in their towns more damage would have been caused.
I now wish to give you an account of who I am so that Your Majesty will grant such favors as you see fit. I am the son of Francisco Díaz, *el galán,* who was your *regidor* in Medina del Campo and whose soul rests in glory; I am also in this city your *regidor* and *fiel ejecutor* of your Royal *Audiencia.* . . . I have served Your Majesty more than forty years because I was in the discovery and conquest of Mexico with the Marqués del Valle, all of which is known to

the Royal Council of the Indies and Fray Bartolomé de las Casas, who was bishop of Chiapas. And now I implore anew . . . because I am such an old servant of your Royal Majesty and my father and my relatives have always served you. I kiss the royal feet of your Catholic and Royal Majesty.[6]

Bernal Díaz del Castillo

Bernal was in a writing mood, for on that same day he drafted another letter, along similar lines, to Fray Bartolomé de las Casas and asked the bishop to intercede on his behalf. He had written to him three times before, but apparently the Dominican prelate had ignored the correspondence.

This specific letter is noteworthy for the praise Bernal gives himself and the fact that he goes so far as to offer the bishop two hundred pesos for religious habits if any of the favors requested are granted. It also shows that Bernal knew Las Casas had a great deal of influence with the king and the Council of the Indies. The letter reads in part:

Illustrious and Very Reverend Sir:
I believe that Your Holiness has not heard from me because I see that I have written you three times and there has never been any reply and I judge that Your Holiness has not received any of my letters. . . . A few weeks ago, being with the Dominican priests who reside in the towns where I have my *encomienda* . . . we had certain talks about Your Holiness and we said that if you saw the good spirit of Christianity and politeness which exists in those towns you would be greatly pleased for much of this is owed to the Dominicans.

You should also see the churches and the rich ornaments . . . of which quality there are no others in the province. . . . And if Your Holiness saw it all how well pleased you would be . . . and I also

[6] Cabañas, III, 353–56.

said to the priests that you would praise me as in all parts they praise me. . . . These priests know and they use me as an example so that other *encomenderos* will do as I have. . . . This I say, Your Holiness, so that you will know about me and that when you write to the reverend priests of Santo Domingo there will come some letters which will favor me. . . .

There is no reason why Your Holiness should fail in aiding me in some very just matters. . . . [Here is repeated the story about Del Valle and the purchase of land as described in the letter to the king.]

I implore Your Holiness to write to the Council of the Indies and persuade them to instruct the Royal *Audiencia* that under no circumstances should it give to the *factor* the rental of the Indians he seeks and that no more land be granted to him within the regions of these towns. . . . Now I want to give an account of my life and that is that I am old and heavily burdened with children, grandchildren and a young wife, and I am in need because I have a poor income; I am *regidor* of this city as Your Holiness knows and am now *fiel ejecutor* by approval of the *Audiencia* and by votes of the *cabildo*. . . . But perhaps Your Holiness will do me the favor by asking His Majesty to grant me these offices in perpetuity. . . . I know the influence Your Holiness can exert and I promise you that if such favors are granted me, I will send Your Holiness more than two hundred pesos for religious habits . . . and I make this offer because I know Your Holiness has great necessity. . . . I wish a long life to Your Very Reverend Holiness and a good Archbishopric, amen. . . . One who kisses the very reverend hands of Your Holiness.[7]

Bernal Díaz del Castillo

[7] *Ibid.,* 357–60.

13   *COLONIAL LIFE IN GUATEMALA*

BY 1560, Bernal Díaz had been married to Teresa Becerra sixteen years and most of their children had been born. First had come Francisco, Bernal's legal heir, then Pedro, and next, Bartolomé Becerra. Clara Becerra, Inez Díaz, Mateo Díaz, Maria del Castillo, and Juan Becerra followed.[1] (Gerónimo, the youngest, was born in 1563.) According to custom, some took their mother's name, others that of Díaz or Del Castillo. Thus Bernal had at this time eight children to provide for. In addition, there were those two illegitimate daughters and Diego, who had moved to Mexico and was doing well on his own.

Bernal's wife, Teresa, was probably over thirty at the time, and his description of her, in his letter to Las Casas, as a young wife may be boasting or may be explained by the fact that to a man in his sixties, Teresa seemed still youthful.

Bernal liked to live well and extravagantly, and with such

---

[1] Bernal's children are all named in the "Pleito sobre de tierras entre Bernal Díaz del Castillo y Martín Jiménez. 1580," AGG.

a family to feed and clothe, it can be readily understood why the income from his *encomiendas* was not always enough. However, he didn't fare too badly according to a report on his properties prepared in 1549 by a certain *Licenciado* Palacios, who was commissioned to inspect and investigate all the *encomiendas* in the jurisdiction of the *Audiencia* of Guatemala. From it we get a general idea of what Bernal's income totaled, how much corn, wheat, and beans he received, and even the number of fresh eggs which had to be brought to his house weekly.

This report, on file in the Archivo General de las Indias in Seville, describes the visit Palacios made on March 7, 1549, to the town of Joazagazapa, of which Bernal was the *encomendero*.[2] Palacios found that this grant had twenty tributaries, and he fixed its tribute at twenty *xiquipiles* of cacao a year. A *xiquipil* contained eight thousand cacao beans, and three *xiquipiles* made up a *carga,* or load of fifty pounds. At that time the exchange value in Guatemala, which was similar to that in Mexico, set eighty cacaos as the equivalent of one *real,* or 640 to the *peso de tepuzque.* This would make Bernal's income from this town come to about 250 pesos a year, although it may have been much less in a bad year.

The following month, on April 6, *Licenciado* Palacios visited, in the same *encomienda,* the town of Zacatepec. For this town, with its seven hundred tributaries, Palacios fixed the tax at two *sementeras* of maize (one winter and one summer planting) of twelve *fanegas* each; one *fanega* of *frijoles* (beans); one *sementera* of nine *fanegas* of wheat; twenty dozen chickens of Castile yearly (this refers to barnyard fowl as opposed to *gallinas de la*

[2] "Visita del Licenciado Palacios," AGI, Audiencia de Guatemala, 128. In order to establish Bernal Díaz' income, Professor L. B. Simpson computed the figures quoted, based on this document and on values as they existed at the time.

tierra, or turkeys); five *arrobas* of honey yearly; thirty *cargas* of chilies yearly; two dozen eggs every Friday; two dozen eggs every day of Lent; and for service every day in Guatemala, twenty *indios de servicio,* whom Bernal was required to feed and to instruct in the Christian faith.

The Indians of his *encomienda* were obliged to deliver the maize and wheat to Bernal Díaz in Guatemala, but he had to pay the carriers thirty cacaos a load, for the road was so rough, Palacios noted, that pack animals could not be used. While Bernal had to provide the oxen and plow the ground of the property, the cultivation, harvesting, and storing of the produce was left to the native workers, as part of the tribute.

Tributes, or taxes, were generally commuted into money values, each tributary being required to pay to his *encomendero* a *peso de tepuzque,* or eight *reales,* annually. This went for the payment of local Indian officials and the upkeep of the town. On the basis of this report, Bernal had an income of approximately 720 pesos and 360 *fanegas* of maize—not the income of a rich man, but enough to keep even a man with a large family from poverty. Around 1560, he was also obtaining about 180 pesos a year from the town of Michoacán, in Coatzacoalcos, which he still possessed.[3]

Since the servants and most of the food—chickens, eggs, beans, and corn—for his household came from the land, Bernal's expenses were restricted to the purchase of clothes, certain imported products from Spain, and, of course, wine, for no Spaniard ever drank water if he could possibly avoid it.

Bernal Díaz could probably have lived in comfort on his income most of the time, and the chances are he did. But there

[3] "Relación de los pueblos de indios de Nueva España que están encomendados en personas particulares descontando el diezmo que se paga. January, 1560," in Paso y Troncoso, *op. cit.,* IX, 2–48.

were years when crops were poor, and there were great droughts which must have reduced his profits. He was not one to save during prosperous periods, and when hard times came along, he did not limit his expenditures; he simply went into debt, so much so that on one occasion his son tried to use legal means to stop his borrowing.

In his improvidence Bernal Díaz was not very different from the other Spanish colonists. After the harsh days of the Conquest they had settled down to live off the fat of the land. They were, in their way, country squires controlling a feudal system. Most of the colonists lived in large houses, dressed in imported materials, ate of the best foods, had servants to do the slightest chore for them, and prayed in churches whose altars were ornamented with heavy gold and silver. They attempted to make of the country they had conquered another Spain, and they almost did.

Despite the comparatively easy life, Bernal seems not to have gone soft. He was hearty and in good health even when he was nearly seventy. He rode over the rough mountain trails to his distant *encomiendas,* preferring on these trips to sleep on the floor rather than in a bed. "After the conquest of New Spain, it was my custom to lie down dressed and without a bed and I slept better than on a mattress," he wrote, and then added, "Now when I go to the towns of my *encomienda* I generally do not take a bed, and if sometimes I do, it is not because I wish to, but because I must keep up an appearance as there are men who might believe I do not own one."[4]

Regardless of where he was, he got up early, and he either had insomnia or, when he was along in years, needed very little sleep, for he wrote: "I can only sleep a small part of the night

---

[4] BDC, *cap.* cviii.

and then I get up to see the sky and the stars and I stay a while in the open air without putting on a hat or covering of any kind on my head. And thank God it does me no harm for I have become accustomed to it."[5]

When he was at home, his life was a routine one, as was that of the other colonists and their families. He was up early and his breakfast must have consisted of a glass of wine and a hard roll, although some of the settlers were beginning to substitute hot native chocolate for the wine. After morning prayers he attended to his official duties as *regidor* and *fiel ejecutor*. In the middle of the morning he and the other colonists took what they called *las once,* an eleven o'clock meal of cake and wine served at home or at a friend's house. Dinner came around one o'clock, followed by a *siesta,* then a *merienda* of more food around five o'clock. Supper was between eight and nine o'clock, after which they sat around and talked at the dining-room table or in the corridor facing the patio. The *sala* was kept locked and opened only when there was company.

Bernal's children probably led a more disciplined life, which was concurrent with their religious training. At daybreak there was the Angelus, then to church for morning Mass, more prayers in the middle of the day, Vespers at church and Rosary at home, and prayers at bedtime. The Church had a firm hold on the community, but the men were seldom as devoted as the women; the men did not always attend Mass, and the frequent disputes between them and the priests continued.

The colonists usually gathered on the street corners, or in front of the portals of the *Audiencia* palace, or in the town square, which was as a rule the center of activity in Spanish colonial life. Here Bernal and his companions discussed politics,

[5] *Ibid.*

cursed the representatives the king sent, talked about dishonest priests and corrupt government officials, and argued constantly about how new legislative measures would affect them.

In the plaza, too, the official town crier proclaimed the latest orders from the king and other news of public interest. We know from prices fixed by the *cabildo* that if a settler lost something of value, he could have his loss publicly announced by the crier four times at a cost of one peso.[6] Several times a week, on certain evenings were held the regular promenades around the plaza.

Strict watch was kept on the young unmarried daughters of the colonists, although the display of feminine charms in these promenades often resulted in courtship and marriage. All marriages were arranged by a formal agreement between the two families after the amount of the dowry had been established. One of the many complaints of the colonists to the king was the fact that they did not have the funds to provide a dowry for their daughters so they could marry suitably.

With the exception of *fiestas,* bullfights, and *juegos de caña,* there was not much entertainment to keep the people occupied. The Church filled a great gap and drew the women to its fold, while the men gambled at cards and at dice.

Yet life in Santiago de Guatemala was not always quiet and peaceful. There were occasional earthquakes and eruptions of Volcán de Fuego, and there were times when the colonists feared their city might be destroyed again. The volcanoes, so close together and so near the city, were a constant threat; the people lived in terror of them.

And there was another fear, expressed more and more openly at every meeting of the *cabildo* that Bernal Díaz attended during

[6] García Peláez, *op. cit.,* II, 136.

this period. This had to do with the old fight of establishing *encomiendas* in perpetuity; the conquerors and settlers, getting on in years, were anxious to provide for their families in the event of their deaths, yet their pleas went unanswered.

The *cabildo* was also having its troubles with Rodríguez de Quesada, the president of the *Audiencia,* who in the eyes of the colonists favored the natives, sought better treatment of them, and advanced policies contrary to the interests of the Spaniards.

When would the crown send an administrator to work with the colonists rather than against them? Were they not more deserving of royal patronage than the Indians? Already the new reform laws were having disastrous effects, they maintained. There were no Indians to work the mines; crops were dwindling and so were tributes. Food prices rose while land lay fallow. There was even a scarcity of corn, for the Indians were planting only enough for themselves. But did the *Audiencia* do anything about it? No, they answered themselves.

The rulings of the *Audiencia* were merely making it more difficult to get work out of the natives. Had the king forsaken them and had he no longer an interest in the welfare of his subjects? It would appear so, they said, for everything was being done for the natives and nothing for them, the Spaniards, who had shed blood and had made a colony of a wilderness. Now if only the king would send a representative who would understand their problems, who would be reasonable and sympathetic and listen to them, instead of the priests, there might still be hope for the future.

In February of 1558, with these thoughts preying upon their minds, the members of the *cabildo* directed a petition to the king urging the appointment of an *Audiencia* president and a governor who should be a gentleman by birth. The document was well worded and the true objectives were not mentioned directly, although it was clear why they sought such an appointment.

This action was timed perfectly, for eight months later, Quesada died, and in August of 1559, his successor, Juan Martínez de Landecho, arrived. Not guessing what sort of a gentleman Landecho would be, the *cabildo* at once wrote to thank the king for this appointment.

In another petition signed by Bernal Díaz and the other *regidores,* the *cabildo* requested that the new president have the title of governor and by virtue of this power have the political administration and distribution of Indians. This appeal was apparently answered, for in May, 1561, the *cabildo* attributed the return of prosperity in the country to the granting of its request. "Dowerless maidens had been provided for, provisions had become abundant and cheap, and both Spaniards and Indians were contented."[7]

This prosperity was short lived, however, and before long the ever unsatisfied *cabildo* was protesting against Landecho as being haughty, capricious, and, even worse, unscrupulous. While he favored the interests of the colonists against the Indians, he managed to fill his own pockets, and graft and corruption took hold of the small colony of Santiago de Guatemala. Nothing could be accomplished without wholesale palm greasing. Some of the colonists became so disgusted that they even talked of the good old days when Maldonado and the fanatic Cerrato ruled.

On May 17, 1561, Bernal Díaz and the members of the *cabildo* felt that it was again opportune to call the king's attention to the question of perpetual rights of Indians held in *encomienda.* But they did so adroitly, by first asking for the establishment of a convent for young girls:

[7] Quoted in Bancroft, *op. cit.,* II, 367.

In this city and surrounding districts are many conquerors and settlers very poor and with many daughters without any help except that given by God and Your Majesty. To aid them it appears to us very necessary that a convent of nuns be established in this city where these young girls may be enrolled; the lack of such a convent has already resulted in many of them losing their virtue and in giving very bad account of themselves. . . . In all humility we beg you . . . to provide the funds required for the founding and upkeep of this convent. . . .

This city is very poor; it has not its proper income; to all other parts of New Spain great favors have been extended in your royal name . . . but this city has been without help for six years and without the funds to send representatives to your kingdon to inform your royal person of all that is happening. . . . One of the things most convenient and helpful in the service of God and Your Majesty and for the good of this republic of Indians and Spaniards would be the perpetuation of *encomiendas*. . . . Among other things we implore Your Majesty to grant the extension of *encomiendas* for two more generations. . . .[8]

In January of 1562, Bernal Díaz and his fellow *regidores* again appealed to the Council of the Indies:

. . . Many of the *encomiendas* of Indians held by those living in these provinces finish in two generations [father and heir] and are then turned over to your governor who has the right to grant them to other persons. . . . While these *encomenderos* and their fathers shed their blood and died in your royal service, they left sons and daughters, poor and in necessity, and it is only just, Catholic Majesty, that they should be preferred and remunerated before others.[9]

[8] Cabildo to King Philip II, in *Isagoge histórica apologética de las indias occidentales*, 317–20.

[9] *Ibid.*

THE SIGNATURE OF BERNAL DÍAZ DEL CASTILLO

BERNAL DÍAZ' SCRAWL JUST BEFORE HIS DEATH

The Ruins of Antigua Cathedral, Where Bernal Díaz Lies Buried

Francisco Marroquín, First Bishop of Guatemala

LA MERCED CHURCH, ANTIGUA, GUATEMALA

El Yllmo Sr. Dn. Bernardino Villalpando, natural de Talavera Obpo de la Sta Yglesi
de Cuba, promovido a esta de Guatemala en 9 de Marzo d 1564, gobernó hasta el d
1569, que falleció en el Pueblo de Santa Ana grande; trageron sus huesos, y fuero
enterrados en la Capilla del Sagrario de esta Sta Yglesia: Se nombró por su suc
sor al Dr. Dn. Tomas Lopez, y por renuncia de este al R.P. Fr. Alonzo Mella
del orn de Sto. Domingo, que tampoco aceptó.

BERNARDINO DE VILLALPANDO, BISHOP OF GUATEMALA FROM 1564 TO 1569

Courtesy United Fruit Company

THE GARDEN AND RUINS OF THE MONASTERY OF SANTA CLARA,
ANTIGUA, GUATEMALA

Courtesy United Fruit Company

THE RUINS, NOW RESTORED, OF ZACULEU, GUATEMALA,
WHERE THE MAYAS BATTLED THE CONQUISTADORES

MARKET DAY IN ANTIGUA, HELD WITHIN THE RUINS OF THE CATHEDRAL

By the end of the year the *cabildo* had raised enough money to send two representatives to the Council of the Indies. Before dispatching them, however, the *cabildo* met, on Christmas Eve, and addressed a long letter to the council. The usual arguments were used, although this time they emphasized that the economic condition of the colonists was such that many of their daughters lived off charity and were about to lose their virtue:

Very Illustrious Sir:
The necessities of these lands are so great that each one of us in particular would like to appear before the Royal Council to testify as to what is happening here, but lacking the financial means for such an expensive and laborious voyage, we are taking the next best method of aiding ourselves by preparing to send two representatives who will act on behalf of us. . . .

In this city and province there are many married conquerors and settlers who are burdened with children which in their great poverty they sustain in their homes. . . . These men having loyally served Your Majesty, now expect some help in obtaining Indians and other favors which this *Audiencia* has denied them. . . . There are many young daughters of these conquerors who are forced to live off charity at the risk of losing their virtue. . . . All this would cease if Your Majesty would suspend the compliance of certain *cédulas* . . . given to strangers and those without merit. . . . Very Illustrious Sir, we, your humble servants, kiss the hands of Your Majesty.[10]

> *Juan Pérez Dardón,*
> *Santos de Figueroas,*
> *Bernal Díaz del Castillo* . . . .

[10] This letter is from the *Libro de consultas a su majestad* in the Municipalidad de Guatemala. It was transcribed by Professor Simpson and translated by me.

The appeals and petitions were futile. The poverty-stricken conquerors with daughters about to lose their virtue were left to work out their financial problems as best they could. The representatives the *cabildo* sent to Spain were no more successful than had been Bernal Díaz twelve years before. Francisco del Valle Marroquín, one of the city's solicitors in Spain, wrote a discouraging report to the Guatemala *cabildo*. "Over these matters [perpetual *encomiendas*] I have not dealt with the Council of the Indies," he said, "because the members of the Council who are there now were put in not as governors, but in order to punish our mistakes; they do nothing for the men of the Indies; and if I lie, look what the *procuradores* of Mexico have obtained."[11]

Things went from bad to worse in the city of Santiago, and Bernal at this period—1562–63—appears to have devoted much time to helping draft letters and appeals to Spain. In the desk of his home, almost forgotten, were the first seventeen chapters he had written on the history of the Conquest. He must have thought of them when on June 4, 1563, he was called as a witness on behalf of Doña Leonor, the daughter of Pedro de Alvarado and the Indian princess of Tlaxcala.[12] In giving information about himself before the notary, Bernal said under oath that he was sixty-seven years of age. He also swore that he knew Doña Leonor to be the daughter of Pedro de Alvarado and that she was later married to Francisco de la Cueva.

In recalling the events at Tlaxcala during the Conquest, Bernal mentioned that he remembered them very well and admitted that he had included some of them in a history he was preparing. He then described in his testimony how the ruler of Tlaxcala gave his daughter, Doña Luisa, to Pedro de Alvarado, who took

---

[11] García Peláez, *op. cit.,* I, *cap,* xiv.
[12] Cabañas, III, 335–38.

her with him during subsequent campaigns. Shortly after the siege of Mexico City, their daughter, Doña Leonor, was born. "I also know," said Bernal, "that Pedro de Alvarado and the said Doña Luisa had two children, one named Pedro and the other named Leonor, and I affirm she is his daughter and looks like him."

He also testified that Alvarado took his daughter, Leonor, when he went to Peru and that on their return her mother died in Guatemala, where she was honorably buried. Bernal completed his testimony by stating that because of the services of her grandfather and her father, she deserved whatever royal favors were granted to her.

Aside from this appearance in behalf of Doña Leonor, not much is heard about Bernal Díaz during the rest of that year, which was not very propitious for him and the other Guatemala colonists. Not only was Landecho's rule as president marked by corruption, but there was serious talk that the crown planned to remove the *Audiencia* from Guatemala, a bitter blow against the prestige and influence of the colony.

To make matters worse, the months of May, June, and July were without rain. In the churches special Masses were held and the Indians resorted to their ancient *costumbres,* appeasing their gods and praying for rain. The drought was so great, Fray Antonio de Remesal reports, that corn sold at exorbitant prices and bands of men and women went about the country seeking work and food.[13] The death at this time of Bishop Marroquín, who had often sided with the colonists and who had considerable influence in Spain, added to the gloom that fell over the country.

Late in the year, Bernal Díaz and the rest of the *cabildo*

---

[13] *Historia general de las indias occidentales y de Chiapas y Guatemala,* 640–41, 645.

learned that in a royal *cédula* dated September 8, 1563, His Majesty had issued definite orders that the *Real Audiencia* should be moved to Panama.[14] No reason was given for the change, but the colonists suspected that the corrupt rule of Landecho was at least in part responsible. The *cabildo* discussed the matter but did not take any action, pending confirmation of the decree and the arrival of *Licenciado* Francisco Brizeño, who was to replace Landecho.

In February of 1564, Francisco del Valle Marroquín (not to be confused with Bishop Marroquín), representing Guatemala in Spain, reported to the *cabildo* that nothing could be done to revoke the transfer of the *Audiencia*. Nevertheless, the *cabildo* got busy preparing petitions and letters to oppose the projected move on the grounds that it was damaging to the province, that it would result in great inconvenience and injustice if the residents of Guatemala were put under the rule of the *Audiencia* of Mexico, and that both the colonists and the Indians would suffer from this action.

The Dominican priests lent a hand to the mounting protests by declaring that without the restraining presence of the *Audiencia,* the natives would be exposed to harsh treatment. But no favorable answer was forthcoming from the crown, only word that *Licenciado* Brizeño was on his way.

Brizeño arrived in Guatemala on August 2, 1564, but there are discrepancies with regard to what ensued after his arrival. Bernal remained strangely silent on the subject. The historian Domingo Juarros, however, records that Brizeño first came to Guatemala in disguise and made himself known only to the prior at the Convent of La Merced, where he was informed of the conditions of the colony and of Landecho's behavior. Afterwards he went to the near-by community of Petapa, whence he

[14] Bancroft, *op. cit.,* II, 370.

sent word to the *Audiencia* and the *cabildo* that he was coming to take charge.[15]

Whatever way it happened, Brizeño placed Landecho under house arrest and fined him thirty thousand pesos. Through friends Landecho managed to escape from the city, and the former *Audiencia* president—that gentleman by birth whom the *cabildo* had requested only a few years ago—secretly fled to the coast and boarded a ship. He was later reported drowned at sea, but this could hardly be true, for in a subsequent letter Bernal Díaz mentions Landecho and protests against the possibility of his being allowed to return to the colony.

[15] *Compendio de la historia de la ciudad de Guatemala,* I, *trat.* iii, *cap.* x.

14   *OLD MEN LIVE IN THEIR MEMORIES*

In 1564, Bernal Díaz was sixty-eight, but he did not feel tired or old.[1] For many years he had not touched the manuscript he had once been so determined to write. His story of the Conquest lay uncompleted and neglected in his desk. If he was ever to finish it, Bernal knew he would have to start to write again.

About this time Bernal brought out the manuscript and reread it. He was aware that he was no judge of a literary work, yet he was impressed by what he had written. It was not as bad as he had thought. In the simplicity of his phrases there was honesty and sincerity. No one else could tell the story of the Conquest as truthfully as he; very few were still alive who could give an

---

[1] Bernal Díaz gives his age as sixty-eight in his "Testimonio de Bernal Díaz del Castillo en la probanza pública de Francisco Hernández de Illescas hecho ante el escribano Juan de León," August 21, 1564, AGG. In a letter to the king in 1567 he says he is seventy-two. This would make him sixty-nine in 1564 instead of sixty-eight, although the statement in the letter could well have been made in error.

eyewitness account of that great event. He was now resolved to finish it.

Just when he had made up his mind to resume writing his story, there came into the aging Bernal's hands a copy of Francisco López de Gómara's *Crónica de la Nueva España*.[2] This book gave a complete and graphic picture of the Conquest along the lines Bernal planned to write. It was an unexpected and discouraging blow. I have already described how Bernal felt when he read Gómara's work. We know the disappointment he suffered and that his first reaction was not to finish his own story. We also know that after many weeks of indecision, his anger mounted at the thought that neither Cortés in his letters to the king nor Gómara in his scholarly *Crónica* gave sufficient credit to the soldiers for their part in the Conquest. They had been lightly passed over and virtually ignored. This lack of recognition continued to infuriate Bernal Díaz and was probably one of the principal reasons why he finally decided, with greater determination than ever, to finish his own manuscript.

But there was still another reason. Angry as he was that he and his companions would never receive the proper recognition, Bernal Díaz, forever the opportunist, felt that by completing his story and sending it to the king, it would be read and receive

---

[2] The exact date on which Bernal Díaz saw Gómara's book is not known. Genaro García thinks it was in 1566, but I doubt it was as late as that because Bernal Díaz himself says, in a preface, that he finished his *Historia* in 1568, which would have given him only two years in which to write it. I have used the arbitrary date of 1563, although he might have seen Gómara's work long before. The first mention Bernal Díaz makes of Gómara is in *capitulo* xvii, very early in his narrative and before he even begins the account of the Cortés expedition. Of course we are not sure that this mention of Gómara was not inserted later.

attention in the higher circles of authority in Spain. If this happened, and he was certain it would, he and his family would doubtless receive further favors and considerations from the Spanish court.

His story was to be more than an eyewitness account of the Conquest—it was to be a document of achievement, a detailed record of what he, Bernal Díaz, had done in behalf of his country and his king. When he said he was writing his manuscript as a legacy which he would leave to his family, he meant it. He was convinced that his story would in the end bring recognition to him and his family. Eventually, that is exactly what happened. Today Bernal Díaz' name is as well known as that of Cortés.

On that day in 1564 when he resumed writing, however, he must have had his doubts. Who would ever read the unpolished phrases of a foot soldier? Who would ever weigh the truth of his story against what Cortés and Gómara had written? Despite these doubts, Bernal went on with his manuscript, now writing with greater speed and facility. He knew he could not allow the years to pass by writing sporadically or when inspired. He had to finish his story soon, for death could easily outwit him. Not many men in those days reached the ripe old age of sixty-eight, and he was fully aware that he was now writing against time, for, as he tells us, he was one of the few surviving conquerors.

The story of the Conquest that Bernal Díaz was determined to finish dealt with events which had occurred more than forty years previously. How could he remember everything which took place? How could he recall such minute descriptions as he was to include in his work? He kept no journal, no day-by-day account—he had only his remarkable memory. But that was enough.

Bernal's descriptions and details were, in the main, accurate;

and fortunately he remembered nearly everything, including the small, human-interest happenings others missed. When he began to write, the years fell away and the past became the present; one little incident led to another until the whole drama of the Conquest lay before him. "Now that I am an old man," he wrote, "I often entertain myself with calling to mind the heroic deeds of early days, till they are as fresh as the events of yesterday. I think of the seizure of the Indian monarch [Montezuma] and his confinement in irons, and the execution of his officers, till all these things seem actually passing before me. And as I ponder our exploits, I feel that it was not of ourselves that we performed them, but that it was the providence of God which guided us. Much food is there for meditation!"[3]

William H. Prescott, a meticulous historian who largely based one of his own works, *History of the Conquest of Mexico,* on Bernal Díaz and who time after time checked Bernal's story with the accounts of others, had this to say about the old warrior's memory:

> It may seem extraordinary, that after so long an interval, the incidents of his campaigns should have been so freshly remembered. But we must consider that they were of the most strange and romantic character, well fitted to make an impression on a young and susceptible imagination. They had probably been rehearsed by the veteran again and again to his family and friends, until every passage of the war was as familiar to his mind as the "Tale of Troy" to the Greek rhapsodist, or the interminable adventures of Sir Lancelot or Sir Gawain to the Norman minstrel. The throwing of his narrative into the form of chronicle was but repeating it once more.[4]

[3] BDC, *cap.* xcv.
[4] P. 504.

Prescott's opinion was expressed long before Sigmund Freud began to explore the unconscious. Dr. Theodor Reik, an associate of Freud for thirty years and a leading psychoanalyst in New York, has this to add about Bernal's memory, which has so often been questioned: "I think the memory of a man of eighty about the years before he was thirty is more nearly correct in all essentials than, let us say, that of a man of forty. We know that old men live in their memories and are forgetful about the present, though the past is very clear to them."[5]

Bernal had his own explanation. When he showed his completed manuscript to two friends and they read his descriptions of all the captains and soldiers who came with Cortés, "they marveled," he wrote, "how I could remember, after so many years, their size of stature, their ages, their facial characteristics, from where they came and where and how they died. To their questions I replied that it was not so remarkable, because there were only 550 of us, and we were always together conversing before and after campaigns and following a battle it soon became known who were killed or who were sacrificed; when we came from a bloody and doubtful battle, we always counted our dead —I retained in my memories all the details about them and if I could paint or sculpt, I would fashion them as they were, their figures, their faces and their manners—I would like to paint all of them, according to life, with the full expression of courage which was on their faces when they entered into battle."[6]

Occasionally, Bernal Díaz did make errors in dates, names, and events. It is surprising how little he did err, for after all he was an old soldier living in a remote Spanish colony where there

[5] Dr. Reik's opinion is expressed in a letter to me.
[6] BDC, *cap.* ccxii.

was little documentation available and few books on which he could depend for source material. His contemporaries prepared their chronicles in Spain, where they had access to letters and reports from the colonies. Bernal had little help of this kind, though we do find that on one occasion he wrote to former companions in Mexico for certain information he lacked.

Bernal has been accused of using Gómara to refresh his memory. But why not? Gómara, sitting by Cortés' side, had taken notes as given to him by the Marqués himself and had probably read many of the reports from Pedro de Alvarado, Francisco de Montejo, and others. It may be true that when Bernal's memory about specific events went blank he turned to Gómara's account and to Cortés' letters to recall them, yet he never copied Gómara or anyone else. Also, as other books about the Conquest appeared, Bernal must have gone through them and compared accounts of certain happenings with those he had written; he found them poor stuff, and those scholarly chroniclers and official historians were often wrong when Díaz was right.

A study of the Guatemala manuscript shows that Bernal Díaz made every effort to be accurate. He not only revised his manuscript several times but up to the time of his death he made painstaking corrections in it. These were not always important, but they do prove that Bernal went to considerable trouble to be correct. He struck out paragraphs and on occasion rewrote entire pages; he was precise on the smallest detail. What did it matter if he had written that ten soldiers died instead of three? Yet to Díaz it did, for we find that he made just such changes. Here are a few examples taken at random. When writing about a certain battle he had said: "... and here they killed two of our soldiers and wounded more than twenty." He crossed out "two" and substituted "one"; he scratched out "more than twenty" and wrote in "twelve." On another page he changed "that day they killed five soldiers" to read "ten or twelve soldiers." Again: ". . . and they gave such great battle they killed four soldiers and Diego de Ordas received two wounds." Díaz corrected this to read "eight or ten soldiers" and changed the number of wounds to three instead of two. "They killed three soldiers and one horse," he reduced to read "two soldiers." He first called the religious figures in the native temples gods, then made careful changes throughout the manuscript so that the word "gods" does not appear, but is replaced instead with "idols." Names and places have often been changed, as was even the color of a horse. In a single chapter, *capítulo* cxlv of the Guatemala manuscript, there are more than 159 corrections and additions.

Bernal Díaz did not make these changes merely because he had nothing else to do. He was trying to be as accurate as he could, for he was by now sure of the monumental value of his work. As he reread page after page, he revised and corrected, doing this even after his eyes had begun to fail him. Why? Because this was no ordinary manuscript; it was a document by which he, as well as the men who made the Conquest possible, would be judged.

The errors he did make were minor ones and those of an old man who had to depend on his memory. He was frequently wrong on dates, and on some events his memory did fail him. In describing *La Noche Triste,* when the Spaniards fled from Mexico City, Bernal wrote that Juan Velásquez de León and Francisco de Morla were killed. Yet in the archives of the Hospital de Jesús in Mexico is a document which reveals that Morla had died before *La Noche Triste* and that Juan Velásquez de León was not in the Aztec capital on that fateful night. Bernal was wrong. But there were hundreds who perished that night; Bernal could not have remembered everyone.[7]

Bernal Díaz knew he was writing history. He had a great fear that his account, if it were published, would be subjected to the most careful scrutiny and that it might be adulterated. In one of his three different prefaces he said: "I must beg of the printers not to make any changes or to take away from, or add one single syllable to the following narrative."

From the time Bernal saw the work of Gómara and decided to finish his own, he must have worked steadily in order to complete his first draft by 1568. But there were many interruptions, even a catastrophe, which doubtless took him away from his writing for long periods of time.

The Spanish colony in Guatemala went from bad to worse. In addition to the serious drought, in 1565 there came a pestilence; hundreds were stricken and many died. This was followed by a violent earthquake in which private residences, churches, and convents were either destroyed or severely damaged. Fray Remesal wrote that many Spaniards and Indians were buried under the ruins of their houses and that the townspeople were compelled to live in temporary shelters or in the streets and that they prayed vehemently. To appease the wrath of God, which the priests were certain was brought about by the scandalous lives some of the Spaniards led, the terrified residents of the city chose the martyr Saint Sebastian as their advocate and erected in his honor a hermitage to which a yearly procession was established.

The friction between the colonists and the priests continued. Some of the priests, the *cabildo* complained, were more interested in acquiring wealth than in preaching the Gospel. The appointment at this time of Bernardino de Villalpando as the

---

[7] On Bernal's error concerning *La Noche Triste,* see the *Anales del museo nacional de arqueología,* Vol. VII, No. 50.

new bishop for Guatemala was far from good news. The colonists were suspicious of Villalpando from the first, and, as subsequent events proved, they were right.

By now, too, the king and the Council of the Indies began to take cognizance of the activities of these priests and on many occasions sent *cédulas* to Guatemala and elsewhere calling attention to their abuses.[8] One royal command to the bishop prohibited the clergy from taking cacao from the Indians and using it for commercial purposes; another prohibited the priests from soliciting from the Indians during Mass such items as beans, chickens, corn, vegetables, and firewood.

In a petition directed to the king and signed by Bernal Díaz the *cabildo* charged that the priests were exploiting the natives for their "own purposes and selfish gains."[9] Protests to Bishop Villalpando went unanswered, while the bitter struggle for power went on between the Franciscan and Dominican *padres*. This rivalry became so serious that many of the Franciscans left the province.

There were excellent priests in Guatemala, and to their credit they toiled faithfully for the good of the Indians, but there were also those who resorted to any means to obtain money. Thomas Gage, an English Dominican priest himself, whose observations are not entirely trustworthy, describes later activities among the priests of Guatemala which occurred when he was there:

> After Mass the priest and the *mayordomos* take and sweep away from the saint whatsoever they find hath been offered unto him;

---

[8] *Cédulas* against the clergy are to be seen at random in any printing of the standard *Recopilación de leyes de Indias*.

[9] In the *Libro viejo*, AGG, dated February 12, 1563.

so that sometimes in a great town upon such a saint's day the priest may have in money twelve or twenty reals, and fifty or a hundred candles, which may be worth unto him twenty or thirty shillings . . . . Most of the friars about Guatemala are with those offerings as well stored with candles as is any wax-chandler's shop in the city. . . . The Indians themselves when they want again any candles . . . will buy their own again of the priest, who sometimes receives the same candles and money for them again five or six times. . . .[10]

While Bernal was working on his manuscript, serious charges were finally preferred against Bishop Villalpando[11] in the form of a *cédula* which was publicly proclaimed in the plaza by the town crier. It was dated August 30, 1567, and read in part:

I the King. To *Licenciado* Brizeño, our governor of the province of Guatemala . . . . We have been informed of the laxity of Don Bernardino de Villalpando, bishop of that province, in punishing the faults and excesses of the clergy in the bad treatment of the Indians and other persons, which has become scandalous and has set a bad example; and while many times he has been given proof of these transgressions, he has not punished the said members of the clergy . . . as a result the guilty clergymen have gone unpunished. . . .

. . . We also understand he has in his home certain women who are not his sisters, or nieces, and that one of them is eighteen years of age and of little integrity and of doubtful reputation. . . . We have therefore ordered the Archbishop of Mexico to send a person

[10] J. Eric S. Thompson (ed.), *Thomas Gage's Travels in the New World*, 236.

[11] For more about Bishop Villalpando, see Bancroft, *op. cit.*, II, 377–78. See also Juarros, *op. cit.*, I, 277.

to that province to investigate and to inform us of the said complaints. . . .[12]

These charges created a sensation in Guatemala. Nothing like it had happened before to a prelate as high ranking as Villalpando. When he was informed that a *visitador* was being sent from Mexico to conduct an investigation, the bishop is reported to have said: "I have received my church not from the King but from God, to whom I am prepared to render an account." Nevertheless, on the pretense of going on an official visit, Villalpando left Guatemala for San Salvador, where one morning he was found dead by his servants under circumstances indicating that he had taken his own life.[13]

In the meantime, efforts were being made in Spain to return the *Real Audiencia* from Panama to Guatemala. The aid of the aging Bartolomé de las Casas was recruited, and he was eventually instrumental in bringing about the change.

Another breath of fresh air came around this time when Philip II, "by the grace of God, King of Castile, of León, of Aragon, of Jerusalem, of the Canary Islands, of the Indies, of the land in the Ocean Sea," bestowed upon the city of Guatemala a royal title:

> . . . Whereas the said city each day grows larger and to make this city more honorable in its service, I send to that city the title of the Very Noble and Very Loyal City . . . so that perpetually and for the future the said city can call itself the Very Noble and Very Loyal City of Santiago de Guatemala. . . .[14]

[12] *Cédula* of August 30, 1567, AGG.

[13] Bancroft, *op. cit.,* II, 378, and Juarros, *op. cit.,* I, 277–78.

[14] *Boletín del Archivo General del Gobierno de Guatemala,* Vol. VIII (1943), 24–25.

A short time before, the king had granted another *cédula* which concerned Bernal Díaz more directly and proved of considerable satisfaction to him. His son Diego was able to wangle from the king a royal coat of arms for himself and the entire family of Bernal Díaz. It meant, at last, royal recognition for the achievements of Diego's father in New Spain; it was no easy task even in those days for an illegitimate son to win royal approval. Yet Diego, who in character appears to resemble his father more than Bernal's other sons, somehow managed it. When a copy of this *cédula* reached Bernal Díaz, he must have poured himself an extra glass of wine, and doubtless his eyes sparkled with happiness as he read:

Philip II, King .... In view of the fact that ye, Diego Díez [Díez instead of Díaz was sometimes used] del Castillo, native of the city of Santiago in the province of Guatemala, and resident of the city of Mexico, in our Indies of the Ocean Sea, have related to me that you are a son of Bernal Díez del Castillo, one of the first discoverers and conquerors of the City of Mexico and New Spain, where he principally served us and later in the conquest and pacification of Coatzacoalcos and in Honduras and in other parts of the Indies, helping to conquer and to settle with tremendous endeavor and at the risk of his life, putting his own many times to the point of losing it ... having brought his arms and horses at his own cost, and as a good and loyal servant, and in accordance with the records he presented to the Council of the Indies, you and your brothers have served us and will continue to serve us.

And as you ask me that the services of your father and your brothers be forever remembered, as well as your sons and descendants, and that your brothers be further honored, we order that you be given a coat of arms that shall have for a background the color of the sky, in which there will be a castle of gold, and on the top tower, an armed man with a sword in the right hand and a shield in the left, and on the sides of the said castle, two lions leaping, and on top of the castle a sun and a moon with four stars of gold and two eagles on the columns of the castle, and on top of the towers two flowers in gold and for the border eight stars of Santiago, scattered in a field of blood, and on top a helmet with white, red and yellow plumes. . . .

Dated at Valladolid this sixth of May, 1565.[15]

I the King

Bernal Díaz, well pleased with these honors, lost little time in telling everyone in Santiago about it. We can readily picture the old warrior, heavy with years, going to the offices of the *cabildo* and displaying the royal order to the other *regidores* and city officials. Then to the homes of his friends: "Know that the King never forgets his servants and those who have been loyal to him. See how he has honored my family and me? Praise that boy Diego for getting it."

As was the custom, Bernal ordered a copy of his coat of arms, with all its bright colors, painted on stone and put above the doorway at the entrance of his home, to be seen by everyone who passed. He, Bernal Díaz del Castillo, was no longer a nobody. It had taken many years, but royal recognition had finally come.

But there was the matter of that history to be finished. He must get busy on it again; time was closing in. His bones ached, his joints were stiff, and his old wounds hurt him on occasion. His failing eyesight made it difficult to work long stretches at his desk. Sometimes, perhaps, he had one of his sons read to him what he had written. It sounded good, even better than he had thought. With the help of a little wine to warm him, along with

---

[15] This *cédula* is reproduced in Vol. II of the Guatemalan edition of Bernal Díaz, which work was published in 1934.

a little patience, he might soon complete the manuscript. Then the world would know what he did, what he saw, and what manner of men were he and his companions.

At this time Bernal enjoyed the confidence of *Licenciado* Brizeño. The governor was in hot water with the Council of the Indies and the king and was denounced in a royal *cédula* for the "little care he takes in punishing the crimes and excesses which the clergy of the diocese commit and in giving bad treatment to the Indians and other persons." His recall seemed imminent.[16]

Bernal Díaz now found himself making suggestions to Brizeño, much as he had advised Cortés in the old days. I can help you, *Su Merced*. I have great influence with the king. I will write to His Majesty. The king will listen to me. Have no fear of that. Did I not get Cerrato ousted? I will see that His Majesty hears all the good things you have done.

Bernal realized that it was not a bad idea to do favors for a governor. Besides, he enjoyed voicing his own opinions and putting his hands into the affairs of others. It would do no harm to write to the king. Had not His Majesty given him and his family a coat of arms for services rendered? His Majesty might well act on his advice. What others were as well qualified to make recommendations as he, one of the oldest conquerors now living?

On January 29, 1567, Bernal sat down at his desk and drafted a letter to the king on behalf of Brizeño. This letter is interesting because it shows that Bernal had learned a great deal about writing during the time he had been working on his history. It suggests clear thinking and a facility in writing which Bernal

---

[16] *Cédula* of August 30, 1567, in Fuentes y Guzmán, *op. cit.*, II, *lib.* i, *cap.* i.

had by now acquired; in fact, its style is so much like his history
that it might well have been taken from his work. In part it
reads:

> Catholic Royal Majesty:
> As many years ago my forefathers were servants of the Catholic
> kings, your grandfathers, and as I myself have served the very
> Christian Emperor, your father of glorious memory, and as I am
> one of the first discoverers and conquerors of New Spain and
> *regidor* of this city of Santiago de Guatemala, I went in 1550 to the
> royal court on certain matters of business. At that time your presi-
> dent of your Royal Council of the Indies . . . confided in my loyalty
> and asked that if some things took place in the governing of this
> region which were not to the benefit of your royal service, I should
> accordingly advise him and for this reason I have written three
> times to the Council of the Indies . . . and all that I have related to
> them was accepted as good.
>
> I know, Your Majesty, that you have heard from certain residents
> of this city who are in the royal court and specifically one solicitor
> who instead of asking for certain things we petitioned has re-
> quested that *Licenciado* Landecho, who fled from here upon the
> arrival of *Licenciado* Francisco Brizeño, be allowed to return. And
> this request is being made notwithstanding the fact that *Licenciado*
> Landecho was found guilty of not complying with your royal
> orders, committing other ugly deeds and distributing to his broth-
> ers-in-law and relatives and others who have no merit large quan-
> tities of gold pesos that belong to Your Majesty. . . .
>
> It is not desirable that he return to this city in an official capacity
> for it would be the cause of much scandal and discord. . . . Know,
> Exalted Ruler, full of so many fine virtues, of what I and other
> gentlemen and priests of good life feel about *Licenciado* Brizeño,
> who came at your orders to these provinces as *visitador* and gov-
> ernor. I say that without any exceptions he is one of the most just

judges in these parts and not even for his father would he obstruct justice. . . . He is a man of great integrity and he has done many honorable things and the Indians pray to God for him, for his help is very acceptable.

I understand, Your Majesty, that he wishes to go to Castile to return to his wife and children. Your Majesty will be served in not granting him such license as he is such an honorable judge and can adequately discharge your royal conscience. . . . Of this I have related to Your Majesty about *Licenciado* Brizeño, all is known by your Council of the Indies. . . .

I am now an old man seventy-two years of age and I give thanks to God that in my days there should be in this land such an honorable man as *Licenciado* Brizeño . . . and if I do not speak the truth, you may order to have my head cut off. . . . Catholic Majesty, I kiss the royal feet of Your Majesty. Your servant. . . .[17]

Bernal Díaz del Castillo

As far as is known, this was the last letter Bernal Díaz wrote to his king. On it appears the following notation: "Seen but no answer is necessary."

[17] Cabañas, III, 361–64.

15 ❧ *LAST TRY AT FAME*

Time and time again we have heard from Bernal Díaz how the opinions of the soldiers in Hernán Cortés' expedition were often considered as important as those of the captains. And so it was in the establishment of municipal rule in the communities where the Spaniards settled; officials of the *cabildo* were elected, and in the beginning they had complete responsibility in running the affairs of their towns. During those early years the colonists enjoyed a freedom they would never have again.

This independence was short lived because the Spanish crown, on its way to developing an empire, realized the dangers. Unless the crown maintained a strong hold on the colonies, there was always the possiblity that in the future they would resist control. The Council of the Indies had therefore created the *Real Audiencia* as a governing body to represent the crown and its interests, although the *cabildo,* or city council, was still allowed to administer and enforce certain laws.

After Prince Philip became king, the powers of the *cabildo* were gradually withdrawn and official posts were sold or handed out to wealthy men as royal favors. Late arrivals from Spain, who had not shared any of the earlier hardships of colonization, were often better treated and given more valuable land than the old settlers. Men like Bernal Díaz were naturally angered by what they felt was an injustice, but their complaints seldom brought any redress. The independence they had seen flourish at the start was fast disappearing.

By 1567, when Bernal Díaz was working on his history of the Conquest, the Spanish crown had clamped down tightly on any feeling of liberty which existed in the colonies. The duties of the *cabildo* became perfunctory and the opinions and wishes of the settlers were ignored. New Spain and Guatemala were ruled by laws made thousands of miles away.

As the bureaucratic system grew, laws were issued to cover just about everything. There was little in which the crown did not interfere in regulating the lives of the colonists, and only because distances were great was it possible to neglect the enforcement of some of these laws. The very representatives of the crown found much of this legislation so distasteful and nebulous that they were frequently forced to disregard royal instructions.

In the archives of modern Guatemala there are still to be seen the dusty and occasionally worm-eaten *cédulas* which the crown sent to its colonies. They cover every phase of activity and even designate the type of clothes the Spaniards should and should not wear. Some of the *cédulas* received while Bernal Díaz was a member of the *cabildo* made these demands: "His Majesty forbids the *oidores* of the *Audiencia* to wear short capes." "All books printed without license and dealing with the Indies must be confiscated." "No church can be constructed without soliciting a license from His Majesty." "His Majesty orders the priests to regulate the use of musical instruments, as many of the musicians, through their music, get to know all of the women in the town, as the result of which they frequently seduce wives and young daughters." "His Majesty assigns to the priests of the various religious orders two *arrobas* of wine each year." "His Majesty forbids that no son, grandson or any descendent of any person punished by the Inquisition can hold an official post."

During this period government positions were sold and such sales were condoned and encouraged by the crown. Some of these official posts were bought for the prestige they carried, though more often they were used as a means of collecting bribes. No better system could have been devised to bring about the graft and political corruption which has ever since remained a part of the Latin-American scene under the fitting name of *mordida,* or "bite."

It was natural under these conditions that the influence of the *cabildo* and the settlers should wane. The letters of Bernal Díaz addressed to the king, and others that were sent on behalf of Francisco Brizeño, the governor, were ignored. But there was yet one voice which carried weight with the Council of the Indies: that of Fray Bartolomé de las Casas. The old Dominican priest was approaching his ninety-second birthday when he appeared before the council and requested that the *Real Audiencia* be returned to Guatemala.

Las Casas died before his plea was granted, but on January 15, 1567, the *cabildo* received word from Spain that the *Audiencia* would be re-established in the city. The colonists had won and lost—won the return of the *Audiencia* and lost Brizeño. Yet he stayed longer than he expected, and not until the early part of 1570 did his successor, Antonio Gonzáles, arrive as the new *Audiencia* president.

In the meantime Bernal Díaz was finishing his history. He had completed the story of the Conquest itself and had only a few more chapters to go. While he pondered what more to add to it, he began to think of his companions, the fate they had met and what had become of them. Sitting there in the shadows of his room, their names gradually came before him. Most of them were dead but their ghosts were all around . . . .

There was Juan Jaramillo, once the husband of Malinche and in whose office in Mexico Bernal had made his *probanza* . . . Jaramillo had passed to a better life long ago. There was Martín López, the carpenter who had constructed the thirteen brigantines used in the siege of Mexico . . . he was still alive and almost as old as Bernal.[1] And there was Hernán López de Avila, who had official charge of the possessions of those who died . . . Avila went to Castile a rich man. And Jerónimo de Aguilar, who had been shipwrecked in Yucatán and later became an interpreter for Cortés . . . he died of *bubas*. There was that soldier whom they called Tarifa of the White Hands because he was not fit for war or work . . . he drowned with his horse in the Golfo Dulce. And that villain Escobar, who was always ready for a fight . . . they hanged him for attempted rape. There was that strange Gaspar Díez, native of Old Castile, who became rich and then gave his money away to become a hermit. There was Pedro Hernández, secretary of Cortés, who died at the hands of the Indians.

And then there was Alonso de Grado, a better man of business than a soldier, who kept on pleading until Cortés gave him in marriage Doña Isabella, Montezuma's daughter . . . De Grado died in bed of natural causes. And that one called Juárez the Old One, who killed his wife with a corn-grinding stone . . . but died peacefully himself. Poor Francisco Martín Vendaval, the Indians took him alive to be sacrificed as they did Pedro

---

[1] For more about López, the reader is referred to C. Harvey Gardiner, *Martín López, Conquistador Citizen of Mexico.*

Gallego. There were the four brothers of Pedro de Alvarado: Jorge, who died in Madrid, Gonzalo in Oaxaca, Gómez in Peru, and Juan, the illegitimate one, who drowned in the sea on his way to Cuba. And Cristóbal de Corral, the first *alférez* in Mexico . . . he was an excellent person and died in Castile, where he went to live. There was Sindos de Portillo, who had many Indians and was quite rich . . . suddenly he gave everything away, became a Franciscan friar, and died almost a saint. And there was Cristóbal de Jaén, who was a carpenter and died at the hands of the Indians. And Orteguilla, the page of Montezuma . . . he also died at the hands of the Indians. And Román López, who after the Battle of Mexico lost an eye . . . he went to his glory in Oaxaca . . . .

"I also want to put in this history," wrote Bernal, "that I came to discover these lands twice before Hernán Cortés, as I have already mentioned, and a third time with this same Cortés. My name is Bernal Díaz del Castillo and I am a resident and *regidor* of this city of Santiago de Guatemala, and a native of Medina del Campo, son of Francisco Díaz del Castillo, *regidor,* who was of that city and who was called the handsome one. I give thanks to our Savior, Jesus Christ, and Our Lady, the Virgin Mary, who watched over me and kept me from being sacrificed to the Indians as were so many of my companions."[2]

With this finished, Bernal next turned to a tussle with Lady Fame, whom he called very illustrious and very virtuous. Before beginning a dialogue with her, however, he prepares the canvas and paints the scene. "Never have there been such men who have won as much as we, the true conquerors of Our King and Lord," he says, "and among these, I must be taken into account as the oldest of all; I repeat again that I, I, and I, and I say it

[2] BDC, *cap.* ccv.

many times, that I am the oldest and that I have served His Majesty as a good soldier."[3]

Bernal's almost vulgar boasting ends on a pathetic note. He has been a conqueror, the oldest of them all, he is *regidor* of the city of Guatemala, but the aging warrior is disappointed, even embittered at what his achievements have brought him. "And I say with sadness in my heart," he continues, "because I am an old man, poor and with one daughter to be married off, many sons already with beards and others recently born, I cannot go to Castile to plead for those things which I need and for those favors His Majesty might grant me for the service I have given him."

Bernal then takes Fame to task for what has happened to him and his companions, and Fame, in her turn, asks Bernal some pointed questions. Where, Illustrious Fame inquires, are your palaces, castles, and escutcheons as witnesses of your heroic deeds to posterity, such as the escutcheons of so many illustrious families attest to the deeds of their forefathers, but whose deeds have not surpassed yours? Where are the conquerors who escaped alive from those battles? Where are the tombs of your companions, those great heroes who fell in battle? Where are their rewards?

These questions, Bernal says, he can answer in a few words: "O Excellent and Most Illustrious Fame ... praised and desired by all good and virtuous men .... Know then, O Fame, that of the five hundred and fifty warriors who sailed with Cortés from Cuba, there are now in the year 1568 in which I am writing this history only five of us alive, and that the rest either were killed in battle or died at the hands of Indians who sacrificed them to their idols and that the remaining few died a natural death.

[3] *Ibid., cap.* ccx.

And if you ask me where are their tombs, I say they are in the bellies of the Indians . . . for they died such cruel deaths serving God and His Majesty."

After Fame has put some more questions to him and Bernal has answered her, he concludes: "And since, Illustrious Fame, I have given account of all thou hast asked me, and of our palaces, our escutcheons and our tombs, I implore thee to raise from now on thy excellent and virtuous voice, so that all the world will clearly hear of our deeds of valor and that envy may no longer obscure their glory."[4]

This, then, which Bernal Díaz was writing, was more than a history; it was the last will and testament for him and his companions. It was also a literary masterpiece that was coming forth from this unlettered old soldier.

Sometime in February, 1568, he was finished with his story. There were more chapters he would write, but the account of the Conquest was complete as it stood. Yet he was not entirely satisfied with what he had written. As he read over the pages, perhaps aloud to himself or to his family, there entered his mind the doubt of whether or not his story was good enough. He was no Latin scholar, he lacked literary style, and many of his phrases had such simplicity that they sounded strange and harsh to the ear. Like all authors, he wondered if, after all, he had failed in his objective. What would scholarly readers think of it? Would his rough, naïve language, unadorned by rhetorical figures of speech, fall flat? He must get men of learning, men who knew books, who knew literature, to read his manuscript and then they would tell him how he had fared.

And so we next find Bernal Díaz walking through the streets of Santiago de Guatemala with the bulky folios of his manu-

----

[4] *Ibid.*

script under his arm. He was seventy-two, and close to such fame as never came to any of his companions. But he was timorous about this next step; he had made up his mind to show the manuscript to two *licenciados,* two men of letters who held university degrees. What would they think of it? What would they say after they had read what he had written?

We know the opinions of these two men, whose names are lost to history, because Bernal told us all about it. He made it a chapter in his manuscript, then carefully crossed parts of it out, but beneath what he crossed out we read:

> When I finished getting out a clean copy of my history, two *licenciados* pleaded with me [here Bernal may be stretching a point, for the indications are that he asked them] that I should give them permission to read it, in order that they might further acquaint themselves with what went on in Mexico in New Spain and so that they might see how my history differed from the chronicles of Francisco López de Gómara and Doctor Illescas, relative to the heroic deeds of the Marqués del Valle.

> I decided to let them read it, because an ignorant and unlettered man like myself always learns from others who know more, but I told them they must not either add to or change anything that I had written about the Conquest as it was the truth.

> After the two *licenciados* to whom I had lent my history read it, one of them who is a great rhetorician was surprised at my memory and how I did not forget a single detail of everything that took place. . . . The *licenciados* told me that my style of writing was as the language is now spoken in Old Castile and that it is more agreeable than the adorned and embellished style used by other historians of these times, and although I wrote simply, it had a certain beauty, because what I told was the truth; they also told me that I speak too much about myself in describing the battles in which I was present and that this should be left to others and that

I should credit other historians and quote from what they have written, and not say, as I do so bluntly, this happened to me, this I did, because I cannot be a witness to myself.[5]

As an answer to the two *licenciados,* Bernal informs us, he recited all the proof he had for what he had written and also showed them the letter about him that Cortés had sent to the Council of the Indies. He relates further evidence to support his story and says to them:

> But if you wish for any further witness, behold the territory of New Spain, which is thrice the size of Old Spain; count the numbers of towns and settlements, which have all been founded by Spaniards, and sum up the wealth which is continually passing from this portion of the New World to Spain. Another reason why I have written this true account is because the historians Illescas and Gómara never mention a word in our praise, but give to Cortés alone all the glory of our conquest.

Díaz next defends the praise he has given himself:

> As to what they said, that I speak too much about myself and that others should tell it, I replied that there are virtues and qualities which we ought never to praise in ourselves, but let our neighbors do it, yet how can men describe battles who were not in them? Should the clouds, or the birds that passed overhead during these engagements, do it? If I, in this history, have taken what credit is due from the captains and the soldiers who were my companions and I gave such praise all to myself, then your reproach would be justified. But this I did not do.

Bernal ends in a splurge of boasting in which he compares

---

[5] *Ibid., cap.* ccxii.

himself to Julius Caesar, even though he admits he is aiming high for a "poor soldier such as I":

> I say that I fought in many more battles than Julius Caesar, and it is said that he was always ready for battle and that when he had time, he wrote his heroic deeds, for although there were many historians, he did not trust them and he preferred to write of them himself.[6]

Later Bernal crossed all of this out and revised the entire chapter, toning down where he was especially blunt and boastful, but he left no doubt about his deeds and why he wrote his history; it was his last try at fame.

There now happened to this history something which is difficult to explain. Bernal himself says that he finished it on February 26, 1568, yet as far as the records indicate, no efforts were made to send the manuscript to Spain until 1575. It may be, of course, that he revised the original draft several times and then gave it to *escribanos* who were commissioned to bring out a cleanly written copy, but even this would hardly have taken seven years.

Was Bernal waiting for those five conquerors still alive to die before he submitted the manuscript to the king for publication? Did he want to be the only surviving witness to what he had written? A more probable reason for the delay is that the Spanish crown did not look favorably upon individuals who wrote about affairs in New Spain without license, and during that seven-year period Bernal may have been seeking permission.

The true answers to these questions are nowhere to be found, although there is evidence of something which may have contributed to the delay. In the year in which Bernal finished his

---

[6] *Ibid.*

history he appears to have been in a bad financial situation; a depression had struck the province and the income from his land must have been affected. We know from the reports of the *cabildo* that trade was restricted, mining neglected, and agriculture at a low ebb. As the colonists had feared, in many cases the Indians had refused to work the land, and the *cabildo* desperately begged the crown for permission to bring Negro slaves into the province.

During this period Bernal Díaz was hard pressed by creditors. We have proof of this in a document on file in the Guatemala archives; it is dated April 28, 1568, just two months after he finished his manuscript.[7] The man who only a short time before had compared himself to Caesar, who had helped to win the vast territory of New Spain, was so badly in debt that he was unable to meet a payment of 350 *tostónes,* or 175 pesos.

Accompanied by a friend and fellow *regidor,* Luis Manuel Pimentel, Bernal Díaz went before Luis Aceituno de Guzmán, a public notary, and signed a document in which he admitted owing Juan de León, a royal notary, the sum of 350 *tostónes.* What this money was owed for is not mentioned—it could even have been a fee for copying the manuscript—and the only thing we find in this *escritura* is that Bernal promised to pay off the debt in the last days of May of the same year. His friend Pimentel, as cosigner of the note, shared responsibility for the debt. If Bernal did not meet the payment on the date specified, "all his goods and property will be seized." Where, then, was his wealth, that he was forced to ask a month's leeway in paying 175 pesos?

By November of the same year the old warrior was in such dire financial straits that he even considered selling his *en-*

---

[7] "Protocolo de Aceituno de Guzmán," AGG (encuadernado bajo el nombre de Juan de León, r, 27).

comiendas. On the second day of that month his heir, Francisco Díaz del Castillo, gave power of attorney to one Juan de Chávez to act in his behalf and to "prevent my father from causing damage to me by depriving me of my rights in disposing of such Indians as he holds in *encomienda.*" Some days later, on November 8, Francisco Díaz del Castillo made another *escritura* in which he also gave power of attorney to Antonio Gómez, *procurador de causas.*[8] In this document Francisco says he is twenty-three years of age, is the husband of Magdalena de Sotomayor Lugo, and requests that Antonio Gómez, as his representative, go before the governor "or before such judges as are necessary to prevent my father from disposing of Indians and land he has in *encomienda.*" Francisco states that he is the rightful heir to his father's property and that he would suffer great damages in the future if the present wishes of his father were carried out. He asks that his father be forced to grant him and his wife "such provisions as are necessary to sustain them."

At first glance this document suggests a rift between Bernal and his eldest son. There might well be another reason for the very cagey Bernal to allow his son to bring this action against him. Bernal was apparently involved in a number of legal suits and debts at this time, and to prevent the loss of his property, he may have taken this means of protecting himself. This is borne out further by another *poder* on file. On February 17, 1569, Bernal Díaz turned over his power of attorney to Juan de Chávez to "represent me in all legal suits which I have now or in the future."[9]

Bernal did not lose his land and Indians, for they were eventually inherited by his son Francisco. Many years later, in 1594,

---

[8] *Ibid.*

[9] *Ibid.*

another son, Bartolomé Becerra, at that time a priest, made an appeal to His Majesty for aid. In this petition Bartolomé, who says he is forty years of age, states that he inherited nothing from his father and that the *encomiendas* in Zacatepec went to Francisco Díaz del Castillo and that his brother received an annual income from this land of at least "one thousand pesos."[10]

After Francisco Díaz del Castillo's action against his father, very little more is known about Bernal's activities. His name appears as *regidor* on a number of unimportant petitions which the *cabildo* sent to Spain, but nowhere is there mention of the manuscript he has completed long ago. However, on March 10, 1575, an inconspicuous note in the records reports that "the president of the *Real Audiencia,* Doctor Pedro de Villalobos, has sent to His Majesty a chronicle of the Conquest by Bernal Díaz del Castillo."

One year passed, and then a royal *cédula* arrived from Spain. Dated May 20, 1576, it contained routine instructions, among which was approval for the construction of a road to the Golfo Dulce. The *cédula* ends with this sentence: "The history of New Spain which you [Villalobos] have sent us and which you say was written by a conqueror of those lands has been received and has been turned over to the Royal Council of the Indies."[11] No personal acknowledgment followed, and if anyone in Spain read the account at the time, he or she failed to comment on it.

[10] Edmundo O'Gorman (ed.), *Catálogo de pobladores de Nueva España,* 319–20.

[11] Pardo, *Prontuario de reales cédulas, 1529–1599,* 28.

16 𝄞 HALF-BLIND AND DEAF— BUT STILL WRITING

On completing the first draft of his *Verdadera y notable relación del descubrimiento y conquista de la Nueva España,* Bernal Díaz must have been convinced that once it was read and published in Spain, it would finally bring recognition to him and to those of his companions who had participated in the Conquest, perhaps even riches and fame, though recognition is what he sought. To be remembered as one of the conquerors of the New World, to have people in Guatemala point him out, not as an aging old soldier, but as the author of an important literary work—this is what he wanted.

But once more he was to suffer great disappointment. In Spain no one considered his story of the Conquest of any value, nor was there even mild interest expressed in having it printed. If his *notable relación* was read or commented upon at the time, I have found no mention of the fact. The manuscript over which he had toiled so long lay buried among the thousands of papers and reports received each year by the Council of the Indies. The only person who realized its value was Bernal Díaz himself.

Before sending the manuscript to Spain, Bernal had a copy made, which he kept in his home. With time and age heavy upon him, he began to make corrections and additions to this copy. He was not satisfied with the preface, so he wrote another and still a third. These three introductions to his work were all different in length and wording, but they all said more or less the same thing: he was the oldest conqueror alive and had been a participant in the Conquest, and all that he wrote was the truth as God could bear witness. Bernal worked on this manuscript until he was eighty-four years old.

The old man, with his boasting and his fanciful tales, was probably not taken very seriously by the younger generation of colonists in Guatemala or even his sons. He was just another soldier living in the past. As his children watched him stumbling, half-blind and deaf, through the house, he seemed to them more of a responsibility than an asset.[1]

How were they to know that this manuscript which their father treasured had any real value? Instead of recalling memories of an almost forgotten era, it was too bad that he had not seized more of Montezuma's wealth, for gold in the hand was certainly better than words on paper—words that no one read. The family lived modestly from the tributes Bernal received from his Indians; there was not even enough money available to buy wine from Spain.

His wife, Teresa, must have cherished with Bernal his hopes and dreams that the original manuscript sent to Spain had intrinsic value. Shortly after his death she tried to recover it from the Council of the Indies and to have it published, but she was unsuccessful in this effort.[2]

[1] In his preface Bernal Díaz says that he is eighty-four and is losing his eyesight and his hearing.
[2] Cabañas, III, 385–87.

Not until many years later did a Spanish historian, Antonio de Herrera, searching through the records of the Council of the Indies, come across the Bernal Díaz manuscript. Impressed by the eyewitness account of the old warrior, he copied parts of it. When Herrera's *Hechos de los castellanos* was published in Madrid in 1601, it contained liberal extracts from Bernal's work. Some years after this, Fray Juan de Torquemada used the Díaz manuscript for source material in his *Monarquía indiana,* published in 1615, and in 1629, Antonio de León Pinelo commented upon it in his *Epítome de la biblioteca oriental.*

It was not until 1632, however, more than half a century after Bernal Díaz sent it to Spain, that his work first gained recognition. Some years previously the manuscript had been taken from the Council of the Indies by one of its members, *Licenciado* Lorenzo Ramírez de Prado, who brought it to the attention of a priest, Fray Alonso de Remón. Remón edited the manuscript and, as they say in Spanish, brought it to light in 1632. This was followed soon afterwards by a second printing.

Throughout the colonization period, books from Spain came to the colonies and were placed on sale or went into the libraries in the New World. Among them was the Remón edition of Bernal Díaz.

Bernal's grandchildren soon learned that their grandfather was becoming a famous man, and they now spoke of him as *Capitán* Bernal Díaz del Castillo, a title which Bernal never used during his lifetime. As a family heirloom, they kept in their possession the copy of the manuscript which Bernal Díaz had worked on and corrected until the time of his death.

In 1672, Bernal's great-great-grandson, Antonio Francisco Fuentes y Guzmán, began gathering material for a history on Guatemala which he planned to write.[3] In his search he found

[3] Fuentes y Guzmán's subsequent *Recordación florida del reyno de*

the old Bernal Díaz manuscript. As he read it and made comparisons with the editions published in Spain, he came upon what he considered a startling discovery: the manuscript he had and the printed edition were not alike!

Fuentes y Guzmán concluded that the priest, Remón, had taken unusual liberties in preparing and editing the edition. Not only had Remón rewritten certain parts, but he had also made many additions, Fuentes y Guzmán claimed, in order to glorify the role of Fray Olmedo, who accompanied Cortés and was of the same religious order as Remón. He said that "in some places there is more and in others less than what my great-great-grandfather, the author, wrote, for I find corruptions in Chapters 164 and 172, and in the same way in other parts in the course of this history."[4]

By this time Fray Remón was dead and could not refute the charges. The manuscript Bernal Díaz sent to Spain in 1575 disappeared and has never been found. Those who indict Remón for altering the narrative could well be wrong, for they use for comparison the Guatemala manuscript, which Bernal changed and edited until the very last. It is quite likely that the 1575 manuscript differed from the copy retained in Guatemala.[5]

Nevertheless, the Remón edition remained for years the accepted version of the *True History,* and all the translations which followed were based on Remón, including the first English

---

Guatemala remained in manuscript until Justo Zaragoza had it published in Madrid in 1882.

[4] *Op. cit.,* I, *lib.* i, *cap.* i.

[5] Wagner, "Three Studies on the Same Subject," *loc. cit.,* 168–69, expresses the theory that the manuscript Bernal Díaz sent to Spain was an earlier draft than the Guatemala manuscript and that Remón may not have made all the changes of which he has been accused.

translation by Maurice Keatinge in 1880, one in German in 1838, another in French in 1876, and a Spanish edition published in Mexico in 1854. William H. Prescott, for his *History of the Conquest of Mexico,* also relied upon the Remón edition.

The Guatemalan government eventually came into possession of the Guatemala manuscript when Mariano Larrave, a descendant of Bernal Díaz, died in 1840 and left it to the government. For some reason the government guarded the manuscript with great secrecy and would not permit scholars and historians to examine it.[6] But the pressure from the outside grew so strong that finally, in 1895, the Guatemalan government consented to have a photographic copy made of the manuscript. This was presented to the Mexican government as "proof of friendship" by Emilio León, the accredited minister from Guatemala to Mexico, with only one reservation: it could neither be copied nor printed.

One again wonders why the Guatemalan officials acted so mysteriously and tried to keep from print a manuscript that was by now a literary classic and world famous. Did they fear that close scrutiny would reveal that this manuscript was not in the original handwriting of Bernal Díaz as they maintained? If they did, no one questioned the calligraphy, not even that able Mexican historian Genaro García.

In 1901, García wrote to Manuel Estrada Cabrera, then president of Guatemala, asking that a copy be made of the manuscript and that subsequently he should have permission to publish it. Cabrera responded favorably to both requests. Before long García began to receive, in installments, a copy of the Guatemala manuscript, which he compared with the photographic copy on

[6] In the introduction to his 1904 edition, Genaro García describes his various attempts to copy the Guatemala manuscript.

file in Mexico. From this work García arranged the text, which was published at the expense of the Mexican government in 1904–1905.

This edition was used by A. P. Maudslay for his English translation, published in London between the years 1908 and 1916 and later condensed into a single volume for popular reading. García reproduced the Guatemala manuscript as closely as he could, without punctuation or capitalization and, as he says, from the *original orthography and as Bernal Díaz wrote it.*

García was so immersed in his task, so positive this was the original draft, that it never entered his mind to doubt that the manuscript was in Bernal Díaz' own handwriting. García's conclusion was hereafter taken for granted, and, strangely enough, no further inquiries about the manuscript were made. As late as 1945, Henry R. Wagner, writing in the *Hispanic American Historical Review* on his study of Bernal Díaz, said: "The original manuscript still exists in Guatemala in his handwriting and with his signature."[7]

The manuscript has always been considered as being in Bernal's handwriting by Guatemalan and Mexican historians. In the edition of his work published in Guatemala in 1934, there appears this statement: ". . . the original work of Bernal Díaz del Castillo is preserved in the archives of the municipalidad . . . it is *written in the handwriting of the author, and the letters are clear and well defined and of regular size. . . .*"[8]

The paleography of the manuscript contradicts such a statement. The letters are *not* always "clear and well defined"; one

[7] "Three Studies on the Same Subject," *loc. cit., 166.*

[8] *Verdadera y notable relación del descubrimiento y conquista de la Nueva España y Guatemala escrita por el capitán Bernal Díaz del Castillo en el siglo XVI,* II, *cap.* x.

style of writing which has continued for many pages changes suddenly and definitely. Even the color of the ink varies. If it was written by only one person, how is it possible some parts are quite legible and others difficult to read? Does this mean that Bernal's handwriting deteriorated as he aged? This seems logical—except that many of the pages written in later years are as legible as the first. None of the corrections or additions matched the script of the text.

It soon became obvious that something was wrong about the Guatemala manuscript. Yet the signature of Bernal Díaz at the end vouched for the authenticity of the manuscript. Could that be a forgery? Impossible, said the director of the archives. The signature had been compared with the Bernal Díaz signature in the *cabildo* records and they were the same.

In order to clear this confusion, the assistance of Edward O. Heinrich, a nationally known handwriting expert was sought. Mr. Heinrich, formerly on the staff of the University of California and whose services were often employed by the United States government, was more than well qualified to give an opinion on the manuscript. Upon his instructions, new photographs were made of many sections of the manuscript. Photographs were also taken of various signatures of Bernal Díaz as they appeared on the *cabildo* records.

Heinrich's studies soon revealed the handwriting in the Guatemala manuscript to be that of at least three different persons. He wrote:

It appears to me that we are dealing with a situation in which the original was to be copied. To accomplish this within a reasonable length of time, the original manuscript was divided among several scribes so the copying of several parts of the manuscript would proceed simultaneously. This was a regular practice of medieval copyists among the monks and friars.[9]

With regard to the signature at the end of the Guatemala manuscript, he made this comment:

This purported signature is a freehand attempt to copy the true signature of Bernal Díaz and it is consistent in its details of personal habit with the writing of the text of that page which lies above the signature. This persuades me that this page is a copy and that the copyist felt duty bound to supply the signature as it appeared before him on the page being copied.

He did not succeed very well. The signature of a graphically mature writer is a highly personalized act. The result is so closely identified that he reproduces a characteristic pattern which is constant over long periods of time. The signature of Bernal Díaz del Castillo is no exception to this rule. He puts enough of himself into his "B" alone to produce something very difficult to imitate at the high speed with which Bernal Díaz was accustomed to write his signature, as shown by the authentic specimen of his signature.

In the middle of the second quarter from the top [in Díaz' rubric], Bernal centered a quadrified design which in its simplest aspect resembled a four-leaf clover. The copyist missed the sequence of the movement and produced a trifoliolate design, or a three-leaf clover.

On the photographic prints of the authentic and questioned signature I have traced out the successive movements of the formation of the "B" and from it one can see readily that they are not at all by the same hand.

Heinrich's findings that the Guatemala manuscript is a copy

[9] Analysis of the Guatemala manuscript was undertaken by Mr. Heinrich at my request, and it was the first time the manuscript was so studied by a recognized handwriting expert.

are further confirmed by the action of Teresa Becerra, Bernal Díaz' widow, when she gave power of attorney to Alvaro de Lugo to recover from Spain "the *original* manuscript written by my husband." In this document she states that the manuscript cannot be printed or sold because she holds the rights to it and that her husband "went to considerable trouble and expense in having a clean copy made."[10] There are no records that tell what happened to her efforts, and although she calls it "the *original* manuscript," it might not have been any more in Bernal's handwriting than the one now in Guatemala.

There is every good reason to believe that what happened is as follows: Bernal first wrote what he called a *borrador,* or draft, of his history. This was probably a rough copy in his flourishing handwriting, with many changes and corrections. He would never have sent such a copy to Spain. He therefore had a clean copy made, and this is the one that was forwarded to the Council of the Indies. At a later time he had a second copy made, probably destroying his *borrador,* which was entirely in his handwriting.

The second copy is the one on which he kept working for so many years and which has his corrections, changes, and additions. However, it does seem odd that his widow did not know of its existence, for if she did, why would she have made such an effort to retrieve the manuscript sent to Spain? It might well be that she did not want it to fall into the hands of others who would plagiarize it without credit to her husband and without any financial profit to herself and her family. Bernal had obviously convinced her that the manuscript had great value.

When she was unable to recover the manuscript from Spain, it is quite possible that she brought out the copy on which her hus-

---

[10] Cabañas, III, 385–87.

band had been working. Because he had not completed it and, as he tells us, planned several additional chapters, the manuscript was unsigned. In order to avoid any question of its authenticity, it might well be that the signature of Bernal Díaz was imitated and written in by the same scribe who had copied parts of the manuscript.

All of this is an assumption, for we have no way of really knowing what happened. To complicate the picture further, in recent years there appeared in Spain another manuscript by Bernal Díaz.[11] This one had a different and much longer preface than either the one published by Remón or the one in Guatemala. On the front folio is this wording: "Of Ambrosio del Castillo, the only inheritance he received from his father." Ambrosio was Bernal's grandson, and how his father obtained this manuscript is difficult to determine, though not of any consequence because this manuscript is definitely a copy made after Bernal's death. But it does indicate that writing had become a habit with Bernal and that he authored different prefaces to suit his mood.

The Guatemala copy remains the only authentic one which has parts in his handwriting as well as his corrections. As such it has great historical value and is of course an important document. The manuscript consists of 299 folios, or 598 pages, and contains more than 300,000 words. It was written on paper from Spain, which came in pads of twenty-four folios. There is little doubt that it was copied during Bernal's lifetime, for the manufacturer's watermarks on this paper are the same as those on

---

[11] This manuscript was found in the possession of Don José Alegria, whose family had obtained it from a priest who died in Spain in 1863. It is clearly a copy and has no corrections. The manuscript has since been published in Spain (Madrid, 1940) under the title *Historia verdadera de la conquista de la Nueva España, por Bernal Díaz del Castillo, edición crítica.*

the paper in the official records of the *cabildo*. The ink used was the iron-nutgall of that period.

Genaro García says that Bernal Díaz wrote words the same way he pronounced them, for example, *augelo* for *abuelo*, *albañires* for *albañiles, gera* instead of *guerra,* and so forth. García also points out that Bernal used his own version of abbreviations, as *alde* for *alcalde, culqr* for *cualquier,* and *tro* for *tesorero.* But as any research student who has handled sixteenth-century documents knows, even the public notaries were not too competent at spelling, and each one had his own style of abbreviations or shorthand symbols.

In judging Bernal's work critically, we must face the fact that he was not the most capable historian of his time. Gómara's book, which he attacked, is actually an excellent piece of work and not a mass of errors as Bernal would have his readers believe. Others even more proficient were Peter Martyr, Oviedo y Valdés with his many volumes about the New World, and, later, Herrera with his *Hechos del los castellanos* and Torquemada with his *Monarquía indiana.* Yet these historians have been virtually forgotten while Bernal's fame, instead of waning through the years, has increased.

Why does Bernal Díaz' work stand out from the rest? He was not a scholarly writer, as he was the first to admit. He was an old soldier with little education, and while it is true that he did not write in the flowery language of his time, this alone would hardly be enough to give stature to his work. There had to be more to his writing for it to have endured all these centuries.

One answer seems to be that in the simplicity of his style there is tremendous force and power. When he describes the cold wind on the Mexican Plateau, one feels that wind; when he speaks of Montezuma, the Aztec emperor comes to life again; when he tells of the fears and anxieties of the men, one suffers with them;

and above all, Bernal takes his readers into his confidence and behind the scenes. He is too naïve to create illusion; he presents the harsh and bloody drama of the Conquest as he saw it and felt it.

Bernal Díaz did not have an orderly mind. He frequently gets far ahead of his story, he jumps around and then abruptly returns to catch the loose ends of his narrative. He repeats himself and often he is as prejudiced as he is sentimental; occasionally he produces confusion when there is no need of it. Yet somehow he blunders through with a warmth, a frankness, and a charm that make his manuscript as readable today as when he wrote it more than four hundred years ago.

Other authors suffer in translation, but not Bernal Díaz. He is good in his original Spanish and he is equally good in the English translations which have been adapted from his work. His style and his manner of writing can be conveyed rather easily into other languages and he is quite at home in them.

He had a decided advantage over contemporary historians. He was in on the conquest of New Spain, and he wrote as he had the right to do: as an eyewitness. Because he was not a professional historian and made no pretense at being one, he was able to approach his subject from a highly personalized point of view, with freshness and candor. He told of the things which interested him the most, no matter if they were insignificant details, and in his enthusiasm he was not afraid to make full use of them.

His great curiosity was one of his most valuable assets. There was little which escaped his attention. His big nose was in everything and those big ears of his heard everything. And so it is that these details which others ignored and which he filed away in his mind and then wrote are today as important to the modern historian as any of the gems in Montezuma's treasure box.

From the very first, historians have combed Bernal Díaz' work for material they could not obtain elsewhere. Prescott found it necessary to lean heavily upon Bernal Díaz and used him as one of his principal sources for his own *History of the Conquest of Mexico;* Bancroft had to rely on Bernal when other contemporary authorities failed him. Archaeologists and ethnologists, digging into the past, have had to turn to Bernal Díaz, as has every historian and author who has ever written about Mexico, about the Conquest, or about Cortés.

Bernal had a good hunch that he was writing, not for his king, not for the Council of the Indies, not for the Spanish people, but for the world; he played his hunch right. It is unfortunate that he did not live to enjoy some of the glory; nothing would have pleased him more. But at eighty-four this old conqueror, with his memories, was still writing and working on his manuscript in a last tussle with Lady Fame.

17 ❧ DEATH COMES TO A CONQUEROR

Like ghosts of the past, the achievements of Bernal Díaz as a soldier and a conqueror were to be brought forth officially recorded once more before his death. In February, 1576, his eldest son and heir, Francisco Díaz del Castillo, appeared before a royal notary with witnesses to testify with regard to his standing in the community and to give an account of the services his father had rendered the crown.[1]

In this *probanza* we learn that Francisco was married to Magdalena de Sotomayor Lugo, that he had five children, and that he was drawing a salary as *corregidor* for the district of Suchitepéquez. There were no longer alive in Guatemala any of Bernal's companions in the Conquest, but there were several close friends who had known him for many years. One of them was Juan Rodríguez Cabrillo de Medrano.

This Medrano testified that he had heard and that it was common knowledge that Bernal Díaz was "one of the oldest con-

[1] Cabañas, III, 365–84.

querors of New Spain, because he came to Yucatán three times," first with Córdoba, then with Grijalva, and finally with Cortés. Medrano also said he had read a "chronicle of the Conquest written by this said Bernal Díaz del Castillo which has been sent to His Majesty."

Another old friend who had been acquainted with Bernal Díaz for more than half a century was Álvaro de Paz. He recalled that he had met Bernal fifty-five years previously in Veracruz and that Bernal even then had the reputation of being one of the earliest discoverers and conquerors of New Spain. But all their testimony, while acceptable, was hearsay; there was not one summoned who had actually participated in the Conquest. Bernal was the only living witness, and he did not testify because other matters required his full attention at the moment.

Some weeks before Francisco made his *probanza* a petition had been filed with the *Real Audiencia* by one Martín Jiménez requesting a grant of six *caballerías* in Izcuintepec, or present-day Escuintla. *Caballería* was a term used to designate the amount of land given to a cavalryman and consisted of about 174 acres. The property in question was located in an *encomienda* held by Bernal Díaz, and the evidence developed later pointed to rather shady negotiations between the parish priest and Martín Jiménez.

Bernal seems to have first heard of this petition for land from the Indians of his *encomienda,* who came to him for help. The preliminary investigation showed that the *Audiencia* had appointed Juan de Morales as *receptor* to examine the land and to make recommendations concerning it. Morales arrived at Izcuintepec, hired two interpreters and named two attorneys for the Indians, and gave them two days in which to make a protest.

In probing for what was behind the transaction, Bernal dis-

213

covered that the attorney for the Indians had written to the *Audiencia* complaining about the haste with which Morales was proceeding. The old conqueror also learned that the Indians who owned the land had been thrown in jail and that their testimony had not been taken. Nevertheless, the land had been granted to Jiménez.

Bernal Díaz was thoroughly aroused, and, accompanied by the Indians of that district, he went before the *Audiencia* and protested the transaction. He furthermore informed the *Audiencia* that he had not asked for these lands to be granted to him because they belonged to Indians who needed them. If anyone had rightful claim to this property, he said, it was he and his children.

On March 12, 1579, he followed up on this personal appearance with a thoughtful and well-written letter to the president of the *Audiencia* which clearly described the intrigue between the parish priest and Jiménez:

> . . . I, Bernal Díaz del Castillo, citizen and *regidor* of this city and *encomendero* of the *pueblo* of Joazagazapa . . . say that it has come to my notice that a certain Martín Jiménez (who is in partnership with a priest called Bachelor Antonio López) presented a petition to your Lordship in which he begs a grant of six *caballerías*. . . . Your Lordship ordered an investigation made and an *escribano* named Juan de Morales went, and the Indians of the said *pueblo* protested, because truly the lands which he demands are where the Indians have their fields of maize, cacao, peppers and other vegetables and they are the navel of the best land of their ancient holdings, and they need them. And, because the Indians protested, the said Morales threatened that if they did not give them up, he would throw them in jail. And now I am told that yesterday, Monday, the said Jiménez made a petition demanding the said lands and

that Your Lordship has ordered the priest who had charge of the *pueblo* to give his opinion.

To this I reply and swear that if the said lands [could be granted] without harm to the Indians I myself should have asked the former governor for them for my six legitimate sons. But, as I have said, these lands are where the Indians have their fields of maize, peppers and cacao, and from which they pay their tribute, and these are their ancient holdings and that is why I have not asked for them, because it would mean the destruction of the Indians.

I beg and supplicate Your Lordship not to give the lands to anyone, because I understand that the one who is behind all this is the said Bachelor Antonio López, priest, and because the Indians, and I, as their *encomendero,* have not been heard. Otherwise they will be destroyed and I shall receive great injury and loss. And if Your Lordship can give them (I know truly that you will not grant them, because it would do great harm to the Indians), I beg that out of regard for the notable services I have rendered His Majesty and all Christendom, if you make a grant of said lands to anyone, you will grant them to my six legitimate sons, for His Majesty has advised that we are to be preferred. And so now in the name of my sons, I protest [the grant of] said lands [and beg that] either they remain in the possession of the Indians, their owners, or they be granted to my sons. . . .[2]

The next day, Bernal pulled a neat legal trick. He had five of his sons (Francisco was absent) sign a petition requesting the land in their names. Nothing more was done until the middle of December, when the *Audiencia* president asked another priest in that region to report if the land could be given to Jiménez without injury to the Indians. The priest said yes.

[2] "Pleito sobre de tierras entre Bernal Díaz del Castillo y Martín Jiménez. 1580," AGG.

But Bernal was in good fighting trim. During the month of January, 1580, he filed more than five petitions of protest with the *Audiencia,* and on February 13, the Indians of the *encomienda* gave to the old warrior full power of attorney to represent them.

The opposing counsel charged that Bernal was interceding on behalf of the Indians because he wanted the land for himself and that this was the principal reason for his opposition. In rebuttal, Bernal maintained that this was not true and that the Indians had contested the grant from the beginning because they needed the land and because what they were using at present was "getting tired." Then Bernal had the Indians state in the proceedings:

> And if our *encomendero* [Bernal Díaz] helps us and his sons the same, it is right what His Majesty commands and if the lands are to be given to anyone they should be given to our *encomendero,* and to his sons, who will look after us and do us no injury.[3]

The attorney representing Jiménez repudiated many of the charges made, but he was not equal to Bernal's activity. The veteran conqueror still had plenty of energy left, and on July 1, 8, and 28, he filed three more petitions in which he accused Jiménez of being a vagabond and of planning to use the land for an indigo factory and the priest of using his clerical robes to further his own interests. On August 12, he ended his concluding argument with these words:

> Besides, the great damage and pestilence which come from the odor of indigo are well known. . . . Indians have died and are dying

---

[3] *Ibid.*

216

from it. And, as to what he says about the Indians not having yet received any damage from it up to the present, I say that we begin restitution of the lands before they suffer it. . . . Your Highness should not permit these lands to be taken from the Indians and given to a vagabond. . . .[4]

The *Audiencia* took no action, however, for just at this time there appeared a serious threat to the country. A certain English pirate, Francisco Drac, as he was called by the Spaniards, was roaming the high seas, not only raiding His Majesty's ships and seizing the gold sent to Spain from the colonies, but also attempting to make other landings along the coast as he had done previously in Panama.

The *cabildo* held a special meeting, attended by Bernal Díaz, in which it recognized the great danger from this English buccaneer, and the *cabildo* records show that the *Audiencia* was organizing an expedition against Sir Francis Drake and had ordered the construction of three ships and five heavy bronze pieces of artillery.[5]

This expedition, consisting of more than two hundred men, chased Drake as far as the port of Acapulco. Here many of the men became ill, and instead of continuing the pursuit of the English pirate, they halfheartedly sailed back to Guatemala. The expedition was so inefficiently commanded that upon its return, the leader of it, Diego de Herrera, was thrown into jail by the *Audiencia*.

Bernal Díaz, alone with his memories, must have wondered, as old men do, if the younger generation lacked the strength and

[4] *Ibid.*

[5] *Actas del Cabildo,* March 24, 1580, AGG.

courage of their grandfathers. Would these men today have stood up under the hardships and the dangers of an unknown land? Would they have cut off their retreat by destroying their ships and then in the stronghold of the Aztec city seized the mighty Montezuma? And driven from the city, would they have returned and against great odds achieved success? Would these lands he had helped to win for his king someday fall into the hands of those *diablos ingleses?* If he only had his youth again and if there were only a Cortés, an Alvarado, or a Sandoval, this Francisco Drac would have been captured long ago.

But let others worry. It was their task; he had done enough. Bernal turned his attention to his own problems. It was approaching Christmas of 1580 and he was deep in debt again. His supply of wine was low and he needed new clothes for the holidays. They were asking fifteen *tostónes* for a *botija* of Spanish wine; he would need at least two *botijas* and that would be thirty *tostónes*. And for good imported cloth—he really needed a new outfit—they were asking six and one-half *reales* a *vara,* which was a little under a yard. He would need at least twelve *varas*.

Bernal examined his accounts. He had land and Indians but no cash on hand. If he was going to celebrate the holidays this year, he would have to borrow the money. And so on the ninth of December he went before Luis Aceituno de Guzmán and, putting up his property as collateral, obtained a loan of forty-nine *tostónes* for the purchase of the two *botijas* of wine and twelve *varas* of material.[6] He was given terms of four months in which to pay up.

Bernal Díaz was never one to worry about debts. As he sipped

[6] "Protocolo de Aceituno de Guzmán," AGG.

the wine of Castile, excellent news came from the *Audiencia*. His petitions and appeals in the name of his Indians on his *encomienda* had been granted and the request of Martín Jiménez denied.[7] It was Bernal's last victory.

From then on his attendance at meetings of the *cabildo* was less frequent and his signature on these records began to lack his usual strength and boldness. Only a few months before, composing a new preface to his history, he had written: "I am an old man of more than eighty-four years of age and I have lost my eyesight and my hearing."

On December 26, Volcán de Fuego, always a threat to the colony, erupted. By the next day it had begun to send up fire with so much fury that the air became heavy with smoke and ashes. At noon the city was so dark that candles had to be lit inside the houses. Then a north wind took away the ashes and the smoke and the sky became clear. But on January 14, 1582, Fuego erupted once more, sending out rivers of fire and hot lava. On the streets men and women confessed aloud. It seemed, one witness said, as if the Day of Judgment were approaching.

It was, for Bernal Díaz. Sometime in the middle of that year he was seriously stricken, for when he signed the *cabildo* records in January of 1583, he could manage only to scrawl out his initials.[8] But he lived until after the *cabildo* elections the following January, 1584, and he either attended a meeting of the *cabildo* or the members came to his home. He cast his vote for

---

[7] "Pleito sobre de tierras entre Bernal Díaz del Castillo y Martín Jiménez. 1580," AGG.

[8] The scrawled initials would indicate that he used his entire arm to write rather than just his fingers. This might further suggest that he suffered a partial paralysis of the right side.

new officers, but he was no longer able to sign the records because, as the *escribano* wrote, "he said he could not see."[9]

He died shortly afterward.[10] He was buried in the cathedral, by the main altar and to the right of the second column, in a place of honor next to Pedro de Alvarado. But even in death these two were not to rest peacefully. A series of violent earthquakes which followed scattered their remains and threw them close together. There are no stone markers over their graves, only the debris of the partly destroyed cathedral. Neither needed an epitaph, Bernal Díaz least of all. He had written his long before.

[9] *Actas del Cabildo,* January 1, 1584, AGG.

[10] The exact date of death is unknown, but it was apparently during the first few days of January, 1584. His eldest son, Francisco, reported Bernal's death to the *cabildo* on January 3 and on that same day assumed his father's duties as *regidor*. See Cabañas, III, 385, 388.

APPENDIX
Events in the Life of Bernal Díaz

1496	Bernal Díaz born in Medina del Campo, Spain.
1514	At age eighteen leaves Spain on expedition of Pedrarias Dávila to New World.
1517	Leaves Cuba on expedition of Francisco de Córdoba to Yucatán.
1518	On expedition to Yucatán with Juan de Grijalva.
1519	Bernal Díaz is twenty-three when he takes part in the greatest event of his life: the march to Mexico under the leadership of Hernán Cortés.
1524	On ill-fated expedition to Honduras with Cortés.
1540	First trip to Spain.
1541	Leaves Mexico and moves to Guatemala, where he is to make his home for the rest of his life.
1544	Marries Teresa Becerra, the widow of Juan Durán.
1549–50	Goes to Spain as representative of the *cabildo* of Guatemala.
1552–57	Between these years Bernal Díaz writes the first sixteen chapters of his *True History*.
1564	At age sixty-eight, after reading Francisco López de Gómara's *Crónica de la Nueva España,* Bernal Díaz resumes writing his *True History*.

1568   At age seventy-two Bernal Díaz completes the first draft of his *True History*.

1575   The manuscript of the *True History* is sent to Spain, but the first edition of it will not be published until 1632.

1584   Bernal Díaz dies in Guatemala.

BIBLIOGRAPHY

Archival Sources

ARCHIVES OF THE CATHEDRAL OF GUATEMALA

Libro I de casamientos de españoles del año 1577 hasta 1612.

ARCHIVO GENERAL DE LAS INDIAS, SEVILLE, SPAIN

(AUDIENCIA DE GUATEMALA)

"Visita del Licenciado Palacios" (leg. 128 [64–6–1]).

ARCHIVO GENERAL DE LA NACIÓN, MEXICO

(RAMO DE LA INQUISICIÓN)

"Contestación por Diego Díaz del Castillo" (Tomo 8).

"Genealogía y limpieza de linaje del Dr. Ambrosio del Castillo Valdés" (Tomo 494).

"Proceso hecho de oficio de la Santa Inquisición ordinaria contra Diego Díaz del Castillo, natural de Guatemala y hijo de Bernal Díaz del Castillo. 1568" (Tomo 8).

ARCHIVO DEL GOBIERNO DE GUATEMALA

Actas del Cabildo.

The Bernal Díaz del Castillo manuscript with its corrections and additions.

"Pleito sobre de tierras entre Bernal Díaz del Castillo y Martín Jiménez. 1580."

"El presidente Villalobos hace envio a su majestad de la crónica escrita por Bernal Díaz del Castillo" (A1 23 1513–496).

"Protocolo de Aceituno de Guzmán" (27–A120 734).

"Protocolo de Juan de León" (25–A120).

"Real cédula en que su majestad acusa recibir la crónica escrita por Bernal Díaz del Castillo" (A1 23 1513–526).

"Testimonio de Bernal Díaz del Castillo en la probanza pública de Francisco Hernández de Illescas hecho ante el escribano Juan de León."

Published Primary Sources

Boletín del Archivo General del Gobierno de Guatemala, Vol. VIII (1943).

Cabañas, Joaquín Ramírez (ed.). *Historia verdadera de la conquista de la Nueva España, por Bernal Díaz del Castillo.* 3 vols. Mexico, 1944.

Catálogo de pasajeros a Indias. Seville, 1940.

The Discovery and Conquest of Mexico, by Bernal Díaz del Castillo. American ed. New York, 1956.

García, Genaro (ed.). *Historia verdadera de la conquista de la Nueva España, por Bernal Díaz del Castillo.* 3 vols. Mexico, 1904.

García Peláez, Francisco de Paula. *Memorias para la historia del antiguo reino de Guatemala.* Second ed. 3 vols. Guatemala, 1943.

Historia verdadera de la conquista de la Nueva España, por Bernal Díaz del Castillo, edición crítica. Madrid, 1940.

Idell, Albert (trans. and ed.). *The Bernal Díaz Chronicles.* New York, 1956.

Isagoge histórica apologética de las indias occidentales. Guatemala, 1935.

Itinerario de Juan de Grijalva: crónicas de la conquista de Mexico. Mexico, 1939.

Las Casas, Bartolomé de. *Brevísima relación de la destrucción de las Indias.* Published by the office of the Secretario de Educación Pública, No. 77. Mexico, n.d.

Linaje, Joseph Veitia. *Norte de la contratación de las Indias occidentales*. Seville, 1672.

López de Gómara, Francisco. *Conquista de México, segunda parte de la crónica general de las Indias*. Mexico, 1870.

MacNutt, Francis A. (trans. and ed.) *Letters of Cortés*. 2 vols. New York, 1908.

Maudslay, A. P. *The Discovery and Conquest of Mexico, by Bernal Díaz del Castillo, Translated from the Edition of Genaro García*. 2 vols. London, 1908.

O'Gorman, Edmundo (ed.). *Catálogo de pobladores de Nueva España*. Mexico, 1941.

Pardo, J. Joaquín. *Prontuario de reales cédulas, 1529-1599*. Guatemala, 1941.

———. *Efemerides para escribir la historia de la muy noble y muy leal ciudad de Santiago de los Caballeros del reino de Guatemala*. Guatemala, 1944.

Paso y Troncoso, Francisco del (ed.). *Epistolario de Nueva España, 1505-1818*. 16 vols. Mexico, 1939-42.

Recinos, Adrian. "Doña Leonor de Alvarado," *Anales de la sociedad de geografía e historia de Guatemala*, Vol. XIX (1944).

Remesal, Fray Antonio de. *Historia general de las indias occidentales y de Chiapas y Guatemala*. Guatemala, 1932.

Sahagún, Bernardino de. *Historia general de las cosas de Nueva España*. 3 vols. Mexico, 1938.

Stephens, John Lloyd. *Incidents of Travel in Yucatán*. 2 vols., New York, 1843.

Thompson, J. Eric S. (ed.). *Thomas Gage's Travels in the New World*. Norman, 1958.

Torquemada, Juan de. *Monarquía indiana*. 3 vols. Madrid, 1723.

Torre, Fray Tomás de la. *Desde Salamanca, España, hasta Ciudad Real, Chiapas, diario de viaje, 1544-45*. Mexico, 1946.

Vázquez, Fray Francisco. *Crónica de la provincia del santísimo nombre de Jesús de Guatemala*. 4 vols. Guatemala, 1937-44.

Verdadera y notable relación del descubrimiento y conquista de la Nueva España y Guatemala escrita por el capitán Bernal Díaz del Castillo en el siglo XVI. 2 vols. Guatemala, 1933–34.

Ximénez, Fray Francisco. *Historia de la provincia de San Vicente de Chiapas y Guatemala.* 3 vols. Guatemala, 1929–31.

Zorita, Alonso de. *Historia de la Nueva España.* Madrid, 1929.

Secondary Sources and Related Works

Andagoya, Pascual de. *Narrative of the Proceedings of Pedrarias de Dávila in the Province of Tierra Firme.* Trans. by Clements R. Markham. London, 1865.

Anderson, Charles L. D. *Life and Letters of Vasco Núñez de Balboa.* New York, 1941.

Ashburn, P. M. *The Ranks of Death: A Medical History of the Conquest.* New York, 1947.

Bancroft, Hubert Howe. *History of Central America.* 3 vols. San Francisco, 1883.

Borah, Woodrow Wilson. *New Spain's Century of Depression.* Berkeley, 1951.

Carreño, Alberta Maria. *Bernal Díaz del Castillo.* Mexico, 1946.

Cerwin, Herbert. *These Are the Mexicans.* New York, 1947.

Chamberlain, Robert S. *The Conquest and Colonization of Yucatán.* Washington, 1948.

Cook, Sherburne F., and Woodrow Wilson Borah. *The Indian Population of Central Mexico, 1531–1610.* Berkeley, 1960.

Cunningham-Graham, R. B. *The Life of Bernal Díaz del Castillo.* London, 1915.

Dean, Bashford. *Handbook of Arms and Armor.* New York, 1930.

Ezquerra, Ramón. "Los compañeros de Hernán Cortés," *Revista de Indias,* Nos. 31–32. Madrid, 1948.

Flores, Fernando Darío. *Antología de Bernal Díaz del Castillo.* Barcelona, 1940.

Fuentes y Guzmán, Antonio Francisco. *Recordación florida del reyno de Guatemala.* 3 vols. Guatemala, 1933.

García, Genaro. *Bernal Díaz del Castillo: noticias bio-bibliográficas.* Mexico, 1904.

Gardiner, C. Harvey. *Martín López, Conquistador Citizen of Mexico.* Lexington, 1958.

Hagen, Victor Wolfgang von. *Maya Explorer: John Lloyd Stephens and the Lost Cities of Central America and Yucatán.* Norman, 1947.

Hanke, Lewis. *The Spanish Struggle for Justice in the Conquest of America.* Philadelphia, 1949.

Haring, C. H. *Trade and Navigation between Spain and the Indies in the Time of the Hapsburgs.* Cambridge, 1918.

Heinrich, Edward O. "Trailing Pen Tracks," *California Monthly* (April, 1941).

Iglesia, Ramón. "Two Articles on the Same Topic," *Hispanic American Historical Review,* Vol. XX (1940), 517–50.

———. *El hombre Colón y otros ensayos.* Mexico, 1944.

Jáuregui, Antonio Batres. *La América central ante la historia.* Guatemala, 1920.

Juarros, Domingo. *Compendio de la historia de la ciudad de Guatemala.* 2 vols. Guatemala, 1936.

Kirkpatrick, F. A. *The Spanish Conquistadores.* New York, 1934.

Leonard, Irving. *Books of the Brave.* Cambridge, 1949.

Madariaga, Salvador. *Hernán Cortés.* New York, 1941.

Millá y Vidaurre, José. *Historia de la América central.* 2 vols. Guatemala, 1937.

Moll, Aristides A. *Aesculapius in Latin America.* Philadelphia, 1944.

Morison, Samuel Eliot. *Admiral of the Ocean Sea.* Boston, 1946.

Morley, Sylvanus G. *The Ancient Maya.* Stanford, 1946.

Obregón, Luis Gonzales. *El capitán Bernal Díaz.* Mexico, 1894.

———. *Cronistas e historiadores.* Mexico, 1936.

———. *The Streets of Mexico.* San Francisco, 1937.

Oloriz y Aguilera, D. Federico. *La talla humana en España.* Madrid, 1896.

Orozco, F. Gomez, *Doña Marina.* Mexico, 1942.

Popenoe, Dorothy H. *Santiago de los Caballeros de Guatemala*. Cambridge, 1940.

Prescott, William H. *History of the Conquest of Mexico*. Modern Library ed. New York, n.d.

———. *History of the Conquest of Peru*. Modern Library ed. New York, n.d.

Roys, Ralph L. *The Indian Background of Colonial Yucatán*. Washington, 1943.

Shattuck, Dr. George Cheever. *A Medical Survey of the Republic of Guatemala*. Washington, 1938.

Simpson, Lesley Byrd. *Studies in the Administration of the Indians in New Spain*. Vols. I–IV. Berkeley, 1934–40.

———. "Bernal Díaz del Castillo, Encomendero," *Hispanic American Historical Review*, Vol. XVII (1937), 100–106.

———. *The Encomienda in New Spain*. Second ed. Berkeley, 1950.

Valle-Arizpe, Artemio de. *Andanzas de Hernán Cortés*. Madrid, 1940.

Villamil, Ignacio Villar. "Estudio sobre Bernal Díaz del Castillo," *Anales de la sociedad de geografía e historia de Guatemala*, Vol. IX (1933).

Wagner, Henry Raup. "Three Studies on the Same Subject," *Hispanic American Historical Review*, Vol. XXV (1945), 155–211.

Washington, H. S. *The Jades of Middle America*. Washington, 1922.

Zinsser, Hans. *Rats, Lice and History*. Boston, 1945.

INDEX

BERNAL DÍAZ

Historian of the Conquest

has been cast in twelve-point Granjon with two points of space
between the lines. Like most useful types, Granjon is neither
wholly new nor wholly old. Designed by George W. Jones,
one of England's great printers, Granjon meets even the most
exacting requirements for fine books.

UNIVERSITY OF OKLAHOMA PRESS
Norman

DATE DUE

JUN 16 '6			
MAY 24 '69			
AUG 25 '72			
OCT 13 '76			
FEB 20 1984			

GAYLORD   PRINTED IN U.S.A.